It Seemed Like a Good Idea at the Time

Some of the Best and Worst Decisions in the Bible

A. Kenneth Wilson

CREST BOOKS

Salvation Army National Publications
615 Slaters Lane
Alexandria, Virginia 22313

Published by Crest Books
The Salvation Army National Headquarters
615 Slaters Lane
Alexandria, VA 22313
Phone: 703/684-5523
Fax: 703/302-8617

Major Ed Forster, Editor in Chief and National Literary Secretary
Judith L. Brown, Crest Books Coordinator
Lisa Jones, Cover Design

Available from The Salvation Army Supplies and Purchasing Departments
    Des Plaines, IL – (847) 937-8896
    West Nyack, NY – (888) 488-4882
    Atlanta, GA – (800) 786-7372
    Long Beach, CA – (847) 937-8896

Printed in the United States of America

ISBN: 978-0-9831482-3-4

Library of Congress Control Number: 2011931206

Contents

୦ᴥ୦

Introduction   v

Bad Decisions

When Perfect Isn't Good Enough: Adam and Eve   1

My Brother's Keeper?: Cain and Abel   5

"What's That You Say?": The People of Babel   9

Short-Circuiting God's Plan: Abraham and Sarah   11

The Look That Killed: Lot's Wife   15

Seconds Anyone?: Jacob and Esau   19

The Champ: Moses   23

"What About Us?": Aaron and Miriam   27

"Let's Make an Idol": Aaron   31

Tongue-Tied: Moses   37

Hot Stuff, For Real?: Nadab and Abihu   41

Stopping for Souvenirs: Achan   47

"Oh, My Aching Head!": General Sisera   51

The Tourist Attraction: Gideon   55

Worst Promise Ever: Jephthah   59

Sorry Excuse for a King: Saul I   63

Point of No Return: Saul II   69

Plausible Deniability: David I   77

Counting Heads: David II   81

Just Trying to Be Helpful: Uzzah   85
A Wild Looking Bird: Nebuchadnezzar   91
It's Not About You: King Belshazzar   95
You Can't Take It With You: The Rich Young Ruler   99
Egomania: Haman   103
A Royal Multitasker: Solomon   111
A Couple of Phonies: Ananias and Sapphira   115

Good Decisions
Chatting With God: Enoch   121
Going With the Flow: Noah   125
Read My Lips: Joshua   131
Swallowing His Pride: Naaman   135
"Go See This Thing Now!": The Bethlehem Shepherds   141
"You Want Us to Do What?": The Twelve Disciples   147
A Bird's Eye View: Zacchaeus   153
Bizarre Biology!: Nicodemus   155
Never Running Dry: The Woman at the Well   161
The All-Star Pharisee: Paul   167
Draw the Circle Wide: Philip and the Ethiopian   173
"C'Mon Over to My House And Start a Church": Lydia   177
Free to Be: The Jailer in Philippi   181
More Than He Bargained For: The Prodigal Son   185
The Eleventh Hour: The Penitent Thief   191

Introduction

⦧◯◯⦤

A young man eager to build his fortune came into the office of the local banker, the richest man in his community.

"How can I become wealthy like you?" the young man asked.

"The secret to wealth is making good decisions," the banker replied.

"And how do you make good decisions?"

"Experience."

Seeing that he was on the right track to prosperity, the young man asked, "And how do you get experience?"

"Bad Decisions!"

*****

I am sure that, like me, something you have done, said or planned that seemed like a good choice at the moment, has at some point ended in disaster—one of those "It seemed like a good idea at the time" decisions. We all make them, and we all pay the price. Those decisions form defining moments that often determine who we are and how we are remembered.

Some of those defining moments may involve large, memorable events such as marriage proposals, weddings, births or deaths. Some events and decisions are so significant that they attach themselves to a person as a legacy—sometimes appreciated, sometimes not.

For example, George Armstrong Custer, although a valiant general throughout the War Between the States, and an eyewitness to the surrender proceedings at Appomattox, Virginia, is defined and forever linked to his ill-fated strategy at the Little Big Horn where he and much of his command were killed. In a similar way, people may forget the many flight records set by Amelia Earhardt, but will recall how she disappeared without a trace somewhere in the Pacific Ocean.

Here are some other people who are linked forever with the good or bad decisions they made: Benedict Arnold—treason; John F. Kennedy—the moon landing; Richard Nixon—Watergate; Bill Clinton—Monica Lewinsky; Abraham Lincoln—freeing the slaves; Pontius Pilate—crucifying Jesus Christ.

A number of years ago, television commentator David Frost came out with a little book titled, *David Frost's Book of the World's Worst Decisions*. In it he chronicled some of the all time worst choices that involved lost money, lost opportunities and lost lives.

For example, he writes, "Sam Phillips had been the owner of a minute downtown Memphis recording company, Sun Records. In 1955, in order to raise cash, he had sold RCA Records the exclusive contract he had with a young man with prominent sideburns who had wandered into his studio and cut a record 'on spec' as a present for his mother. RCA paid Mr. Phillips the not inconsiderable sum of $35,000, but, even as he pocketed the check, he was forfeiting all his royalties on more than a billion records—one for every four people on the earth." The young man with the sideburns was Elvis Presley.

In the middle of the Depression two struggling illustrators, Joe Schuster and Jerry Seigel, anxious to make some money on a seemingly minor cartoon, sold the complete rights to their character for $130—$65 each. And on June 1, 1938, Action Comics published the first in a long series of the adventures of their new acquisition—Superman.

David Frost goes on, "The tale is told about Lana Turner's grandfather, who owned a half share in a small firm which made a soft drink called Coca-Cola. Despairing of a product burdened with so unappealing a name, he sold out. He had not, however, lost faith in the soft drink business, so he invested the proceeds in a firm he deemed more likely to flourish—the Raspberry Cola Company."

But that tale of woe does not end there, "for a few years later the Coca-Cola Company, which in the meantime had done better than its one-time co-owner had anticipated, was offered the twice-bankrupt Pepsi-Cola Company. Its then owner, Charles Guft, was willing to let his subsidiary go for a mere $1,000. But with an overconfidence born of their virtual monopoly of the soft drink business, Coca-Cola spurned the offer, thus missing the opportunity to remove the business that would in due course become its arch rival."

According to Frost, not all bad decisions involve money. During the Battle of the Wilderness, Union General John Sedgwick "was inspecting his troops and standing gazing out over a parapet. His officers urged him to duck down, but the general had scant respect for the enemy and decided to ignore the warnings. 'Nonsense,' he declared. 'They couldn't hit an elephant at this dist . . .'" as he took a lethal bullet in the head from a Confederate soldier.

Some bad decisions involve an arrogance that affects many. "In November 1888 the Committee of the South Fork Fishing and Hunting Clubs in the Allegheny Mountains of Pennsylvania decided, yet again, to reject an appeal from the Cambria Iron Company to repair the dam that kept the South Fork Reservoir filled. The sluice gates must never be opened, they argued, since to do so would disturb both the fish and the tranquility so valued by the rich members of the club, many of whom belonged to the best families in Pittsburgh. On May 31, 1889, a freak rainstorm filled the lake to its utmost capacity. At 3:10 p.m. the dam gave way and a wall of water swept into Johnstown. Twenty-two hundred people, including many Fishing and Hunting Club members, were drowned."

Some decisions have no ulterior motive or plan for personal gain. They just happen and often with unforeseen consequences, much like Isaac Newton's "Third Law of Motion" that says: "For every action, there is an equal and opposite reaction." Sometimes the reaction, although opposite, is far greater than equal.

Such was the case for New York Yankee first-baseman, Wally Pipp. Suffering from a headache, he decided to take a couple of aspirins and a day off from baseball to recuperate. The Yankees played Pipp's backup player, who stayed for 2,130 consecutive games until health finally forced him to take himself out of the lineup. Few people remember Wally Pipp and his extraordinarily expensive headache, while even the most casual baseball fan knows of Lou Gehrig.

As in Frost's book, there are many terrible decisions recounted in the pages of the Bible. Some affected an individual or a small circle of people, while others created problems we have had to face for millennia. This book includes some examples of them. Perhaps a few of your all-time worst decisions come close to the ones included here, but just as true, there are also good decisions included that have brought life, security and hope.

When Perfect Isn't Good Enough

Adam and Eve

The creation story in Genesis describes the universe as beginning "without form and void," and then being filled with stars, planets, clouds, animals, plants and people. The last creations in the Lord's burst of divine exuberance were Adam and Eve, with Adam being made from the dust of the ground and Eve fashioned from a rib taken from Adam's side in the most glorious bit of surgery ever recorded.

The Lord designed a fabulous garden and placed the newly-created man and woman in it, where they would be safe and happy with freedom to grow in their love for Him and for each other. They had no obligations, no aches or pains, no in-laws, no rowdy neighbors, no mortgage payments and no problems. They didn't have to get up and go to work, fight the traffic or do anything other than get to know each other and spend each day with God. Imagine having the opportunity to walk and talk with God, seeing Him and hearing His voice! Perfect.

In the middle of the garden stood the tree of the knowledge of good and evil. Adam and Eve could eat anything they liked, but the Lord commanded, "You must not eat from the tree of the knowledge of good and evil, for when you eat of it you will surely die" (Gen. 2:8,16–17). In fact, the only rule the Lord gave to the first pair in Eden was to leave that one tree alone. Everything else was available to use and enjoy. But even as the happy couple spent their days having fun with God and each other, sin prowled paradise, looking for a way to ruin everything.

CURIOSITY

One day when Eve was alone, perhaps while Adam was naming the animals and trying to decide what to call the odd-looking hippo, the serpent said to her, "Did God really say, 'You must not eat from any tree in the garden?'" (3:1). The serpent created doubt, and with that doubt a potentially lethal curiosity.

Volunteering more information than she should have, Eve said, "We may eat fruit from the trees in the garden, but God did say, 'You must not eat from the fruit that is in the middle of the garden, and you must not touch it, or you will die'" (3:2). Eve knew there was something dangerous about that banned tree and she wanted to avoid it.

"No, that's not what happens," the serpent hissed. "You won't die. God wants to keep you down because if you eat from that tree you'll be just as He is, able to know both good and evil." Adam and Eve had known only simple innocence and God's tender provision and had no idea anyone would try to harm them or subvert the truth.

Perhaps thinking that God and Adam would be pleased with her initiative, Eve ate some of the fruit (3:6). "Hey, Adam," she probably shouted to her husband, "this is great. Try it." And Adam ate—willingly, eagerly, without the slightest hesitation since "it seemed like a good idea at the time."

Immediately their eyes were opened, they knew they had done wrong and they felt shame for the first time. They looked at each other and at themselves and realized that they were naked. Embarrassed, Adam and Eve tried to sew fig leaves together to cover themselves in the world's worst fashion fix. Along with poor fashion, now they had to bear the brutal awareness of sin and disobedience.

THE PRICE

Adam and Eve had to deal with the consequences of breaking God's prime directive. They died a spiritual death, corrupting the imago dei and spoiling an intimacy with God that would never fully be restored. Once sin was turned loose on the world, there was no going back and the deed could not be canceled out. But although sin could not be undone, God would one day make a provision through His Son Jesus for sinful, weak, stubborn, self-willed mankind to be forgiven.

The Lord could have looked the other way and given Adam and Eve a second shot at things—golfers call it "taking a mulligan." Had He done that, though, God would not be God, for if He is loving, He must be just. If He rewards righteousness, He must also punish sin and rebellion. So the Lord said to the serpent, "Because you have done this, cursed are you above all the livestock and all the wild animals! You will crawl on your belly and you will eat dust all the days of your life. And I will put enmity between you and the woman, and between your offspring and hers; he will crush your head, and you will strike his heel" (3:14–15). The serpent would spend his life hating and being hated.

To Eve, God said, "I will greatly increase your pains in childbearing; with pain you will give birth to children. Your desire will be for your husband, and he will rule over you" (3:16). She would be fated to look to her husband for communication and intimacy, and he, no doubt, would learn to ignore her pleas for meaningful conversation and emotional comfort long before the invention of football and television.

To Adam, God said, "Because you listened to your wife and ate from the tree about which I commanded you . . . cursed is the ground because of you; through painful toil you will eat of it all the days of your life. It will produce thorns and thistles for you, and you will eat the plants of the field. By the sweat of your brow you will eat your food until you return to the ground, since from it you were taken; for dust you are and to dust you will return" (3:17–19). So if you hate to go to work each day, blame Adam.

GOD'S SENTENCE

Now they would be exposed to the searing heat of the sun, the aches and pains of labor, and an inevitable sentence of death filled with anxiety and heartbreak. Adam and Eve had placed themselves squarely in the path of God's stern correction. What could the Lord do with them now that they had experienced evil along with good? He couldn't just leave them in the garden in their sinful state. God said, "The man has now become like one of us, knowing good and evil. He must not be allowed to reach out his hand and take also from the tree of life and eat, and live forever" (3:22). To keep them from getting into more trouble, the Lord banished Adam and Eve from the garden and positioned an angel with a flaming sword by the exit to bar them from returning (3:23–24).

For bringing sin into the world, the punishment had to be severe and decisive. Besides, God's greatest concern was that Adam and Eve would eat from the tree of life and live forever in their defiled state without hope of even the rest that comes with death. Can you imagine what would have happened had they eaten that fruit? They would still be here—two wrinkled, shriveled, nasty old people consumed by their bitterness.

Adam and Eve were "outsiders" and knew there was nothing they could say or do to make the situation right. They lost the ability to find their way back to where they had been in their relationship with God and each other. What a high price to pay for fruit and an education!

My Brother's Keeper?

Cain and Abel

⁂

Children bless us beyond measure and often complicate our lives beyond belief. We know that Adam and Eve's first set of children were Cain and his younger brother Abel. Their names are recorded in Genesis 4:1–2: "Adam lay with his wife Eve, and she became pregnant and gave birth to Cain. She said, 'With the help of the Lord I have brought forth a man.' Later she gave birth to his brother Abel. Now Abel kept flocks, and Cain worked the soil." From that single reference we know the parents, how the children were conceived, their birth order and their occupations.

I feel sorry, though, for Adam and his family. I cannot imagine the unrelenting tension of Mom and Dad fighting over who was tempted first or whose fault it was that they had been kicked out of Eden. Every night, with years lengthening into decades, and decades into centuries, sin's poison worked its way into memories and beliefs, making Adam and Eve and their family more and more miserable.

We know very little of Cain and Abel except for their occupations. Cain, the farmer, worked the ground that the Lord had cursed. Perhaps Cain may have felt that he deserved to stay in Eden because it was his parents who had ruined everything, not him.

Was Abel the "good son," the one Cain deeply resented and with whom he was unfavorably compared? Did Abel remember Eden and long to keep part of that memory alive? Was he just glad to have the opportunity for a relationship with God—no matter how remote or fragile?

In the same way, did Cain dwell on what they once had in Eden and grow more and more bitter and resentful?

TWO GIFTS

Scripture records that as the brothers grew older, Cain brought some of his vegetables as an offering to the Lord, while Abel brought choice cuts of meat from some of his flock. The Lord was pleased with Abel and his offering, but not with Cain and his gift. Why was Abel's offering accepted and not Cain's? Some have suggested that Abel's gift was a blood offering of the sinless for the guilty, as an object lesson in anticipation of Christ's atoning death on the cross.

In Hebrews 11:4 we read, "By faith Abel offered God a better sacrifice than Cain did. By faith he was commended as a righteous man, when God spoke well of his offerings. And by faith he still speaks, even though he is dead."

Abel's sacrifice was superior because it was offered in faith. Because he trusted and loved God, Abel thought that only his best offering would be suitable, and that God would respond in kind. As of yet there was no codified standard for an acceptable offering. That would come much later, as Moses wrote down God's Law instructing Israel on how to worship.

It is hard to imagine God looking with disdain on anyone's best offering. He would not hold a shepherd in higher regard than a farmer, or value a corporate executive more than an auto mechanic. He expects a willing heart and a positive attitude, genuine regret for sin and an equally genuine desire for forgiveness, all with a spirit thankful for His provision and care. Cain's offering was rejected because his heart was not right. If the heart is right, then the motives are right, the worship is right, and the offering is accepted. Break that chain and the offering is just another bushel of spuds.

God would have gladly helped Cain had he asked, but Cain's bitterness would not allow him to show any weakness. Then the Lord said to Cain, "Why are you angry? Why is your face downcast? If you do what is right, will you not be accepted? But if you do not do what is right, sin is crouching at your door; it desires to have you, but you must master it" (4:3–7). God wanted Cain to deal with his attitude problem before it was too late.

One day, when Cain finally reached his breaking point, he said to Abel, "Let's go out to the field" (4:8). Although not directly stated, the biblical account makes it clear that Cain committed premeditated murder, not a crime of anger or passion. Cain lured Abel out into the fields, away from any witnesses, with the single intent of getting rid of his hated little brother.

"WHAT HAVE YOU DONE?"

The Lord asked Cain, "Where is your brother, Abel?"—a question much like most parents ask, not for information but to elicit a reaction. Cain responded with an icy, "I don't know. Am I my brother's keeper?" although he knew exactly where Abel was and what had happened to him.

"What have you done?" the Lord asked. God knew exactly what had happened but needed to see if Cain fully appreciated the effect of his actions. "Your brother's blood cries out to me from the ground" (4:10). "I know what you did," the Lord continued. "Don't think you got away with it. You will be driven from this land, for it reeks of your brother's freshly-spilled blood. You will work the land but it will not grow crops for you, no matter what you do. You will have no place to call your own and will be a restless wanderer on the earth" (4:12).

Cain broke down when confronted with his punishment. He didn't care that Abel was dead, or that God was angry, or that his parents would grieve the loss of their son. But the thought of his own mortality terrified him: "Whoever finds me will kill me" (4:14). He may have thought that subsequent sons born to Adam and Eve would spend their lives hunting him down and then kill him. We do not know the age of Cain or Abel at the time of the murder, but perhaps Cain had the emotional maturity of a teenager who had not yet made the connection between actions and consequences.

Life is sacred to God, so murder is not something that could be allowed to fade away. Cain had to take his punishment. Yet, in a characteristic display of grace, the Lord marked Cain with a warning that anyone who harmed him would be killed, and that person's family would suffer revenge seven times over. The mark must have been as easy to spot as a person wearing a clown suit walking around downtown at high noon.

We would like to think that our actions and decisions are ours alone. But in reality, our choices, especially where sin and rebellion against God are concerned, most often influence our children and spawn consequences from one generation to the next. Abel may have been the first to die at the hands of another, but he was certainly not the last.

"What's That You Say?"

The People of Babel

එ⊙⊙ඁ

L ong after the fiascos with Adam and Eve and Cain and Abel, the growing clan from Shinar embarked on an unprecedented building campaign that culminated in the city of Babel: "Come, let us build our-selves a city, with a tower that reaches to the heavens, so that we may make a name for ourselves and not be scattered over the face of the whole earth" (Gen. 11:4). The people's goal was not to build a tower to reach heaven in order to see God and worship Him, but rather to verify their belief that He wasn't there at all. The citizens of Babel, originators of secular humanism, wanted to deify man, not God. If they could prove there was no God, they could tout themselves as the supreme creative force in the universe. Eager to promote this concept, they were more than willing to risk cutting themselves adrift from the Lord in order to proclaim their findings while ridiculing God's faithful followers.

The Lord came down to see the city and the tower they were build-ing ... [and] said, "If as one people speaking the same language they have begun to do this, then nothing they plan to do will be impossible for them'" (11:5–6).

BROKENNESS

To remedy the situation the Lord decided to confuse Babel's language so the people could not understand each other, which halted the construction of the tower and the city. Some groups were still able to communicate with each other—or else they would all have resorted to grunts, hand gestures, and strange noises. People gravitated to those they could understand and who understood them, thus scattering to different areas. As the people moved apart, God knew there would be less potential for short-term rebellion against Him.

Does our society obey any better than the people of Babel, as we promote our own agendas instead of God's will for His kingdom? Even though we may speak the same language, we still face a huge challenge in communicating with our spouses, our children, our friends and co-workers. We get angry and yell and we are often unheard and misunderstood, so we resort to small talk about weather or sports. Thanks to the chaos at Babel, we seem fated not to express the deep longings of our hearts and souls, until that loss drives home our need to communicate with God—the only One who truly hears and understands even the deep groans and sighs too painful to put into words.

What the Lord confused at Babel, however, He clarified with the gift of the Holy Spirit at Pentecost as recorded in Acts 2:1–12. At Pentecost, rather than hearing a cacophony, the people listened to the life-changing gospel preached in their own language, believed the message and received new life in Christ.

Most of us have trouble communicating with those we love the most, especially our kids. Thanks to the folks at Babel, we are still paying the price for that terrible decision—speaking but not communicating, talking but often not being fully understood.

Short-Circuiting God's Plan
Abraham and Sarah

ᘀᘒᘙ

A braham—the father of three major religions, believer in One God in a polytheistic society—is described in the Bible as a prototype of faith. Because he obediently left his home in Ur of Chaldea to go where the Lord sent him, God promised that he and his wife, Sarah, who were childless, would have a son and heir. The Lord also promised that Abraham's offspring would be as numerous as the stars (Gen. 15:5). Abraham (originally Abram) accepted God at His word, and the Lord recognized that faith, simple and rudimentary, as righteousness.

The Lord declared, "Your name will be Abraham, for I have made you a father of many nations. I will make you very fruitful; I will make nations of you, and kings will come from you. I will establish my covenant as an everlasting covenant between me and you and your descendants after you for the generations to come, to be your God and the God of your descendants . . ." (17:4–7).

Sarah (originally Sarai) had a plan that she hoped would expedite God's fulfillment of His pledge. She made a decision that was quick, decisive and wrong. Since the Lord was not moving quickly to give her a son and heir, her impatience drove her to take matters into her own hands.

HAGAR

Sarai suggested that Abram have sexual relations with her Egyptian maidservant, Hagar: "Perhaps I can build a family through her" (16:2).

Abram agreed and Hagar conceived a child, putting Abram and Sarai on their way to having a family and heir, only not the way God had promised. When Hagar became pregnant—and probably pampered by Abram—she began to ridicule and "despise her mistress" (16:4). It is also quite likely that Hagar mocked Sarai for her inability to have children, since in those days infertility carried an appalling social stigma.

Hagar's attitude provoked Sarai to shout angrily at Abram, "You are responsible for the wrong I am suffering. I put my servant in your arms, and now that she knows she is pregnant, she despises me. May the Lord judge between you and me" (16:5).

Abram replied, "Your servant is in your hands . . . Do with her whatever you think best" (16:6). So Sarai greatly mistreated Hagar until Hagar ran away. Then an angel of the Lord found her alone by a desert spring along the road to Shur, out in the middle of nowhere. When the angel asked Hagar to explain what she was doing, she obviously had no plan or destination in mind. The angel told her, "'Go back to your mistress and submit to her.' The angel added, 'I will so increase your descendants that they will be too numerous to count . . . You will have a son. You shall name him Ishmael, for the Lord has heard of your misery'" (16:9–11). The angel added a promise that sounded more like a curse than a blessing: "He will be a wild donkey of a man; his hand will be against everyone and everyone's hand against him, and he will live in hostility toward all his brothers" (16:12).

The Lord also had news for Sarai. Her name would be changed to Sarah—a name worthy of the mother of nations and kings (17:15–16). This time Abraham trusted the Lord's plan, although at his age he had to laugh thinking about diapers, around-the-clock feedings, toilet training and the "terrible twos." Abraham wondered, *Will a son be born to a man 100 years old? Will Sarah bear a child at the age of 90?*"

COVENANT

God answered Abraham's question with a promise: "Your wife Sarah will bear you a son, and you will call him Isaac. I will establish my covenant with him as an everlasting covenant for his descendants after him. And as for Ishmael, I have heard you: I will surely bless him; I will make him fruitful and will greatly increase his numbers. He will be the father of twelve rulers, and I will make him into a great nation. But my covenant I will establish with Isaac, whom Sarah will bear to you by this time next year "(17:19–21).

The Lord contacted Abraham once again while the old patriarch sat in front of his tent in the shade of the great trees of Mamre. Abraham looked up and saw three men who had not been there just moments before. As soon as he saw them, he hurried to meet them, bowing low to the ground. To welcome them, he provided water to wash their feet (18:2–5). They agreed to stay awhile, and Abraham asked Sarah to serve some of her delicious bread, hot from the oven, to make a good impression on their angelic guests. While they were eating, the visitors asked, "Where is your wife Sarah?" (18:9). Abraham indicated that she was in the family tent nearby. Then the angel of the Lord restated the promise of a son and heir. He informed Abraham that Sarah would have a baby by the same time next year. Thinking she was out of earshot, Sarah chuckled at the thought of becoming a mother at her age. She thought the prospect wildly hilarious—the angel did not. He asked Abraham, "Why did Sarah laugh? . . . Is anything too hard for the Lord? I will return to you at the appointed time next year and Sarah will have a son" (18:13–14).

SON OF LAUGHTER

Sarah was afraid. How could he have heard me laugh unless he was truly sent by God, she wondered. When confronted, she denied it. But the angelic visitors insisted, "You most certainly did laugh, and you know we heard it" (18:15). So, Abraham and Sarah's son would be named Isaac—son of laughter—to remind his aging parents of their cynical attitude. They were learning, though, that the Lord can and will accomplish what He sets out to do—with or without our cooperation. He prefers, however, that we are willing, and willing to do it His way.

Had Abraham and Sarah shown more trust and obedience, the covenant would have been completed in the Lord's way and in His time. By taking matters into their own hands, they created a rivalry and an animosity that has lasted for centuries with no apparent end in sight. Descendants and adherents of three great religions are still fighting each other in the same land that should have been a place of peace and cooperation.

The Look
That Killed
Lot's Wife

A braham's extended family soon grew so large that the surrounding countryside could not support the population of people, flocks and herds. The time had come for Abraham and his nephew, Lot, to separate so that they could both build a home and a future without getting in each other's way. Quarreling had erupted between the two families and the Canaanites who still lived in the area.

Abraham, by nature a peacemaker, said to Lot, "Let's part company. If you go to the left, I'll go to the right; if you go to the right, I'll go to the left" (Gen. 13:8–9). Abraham divided the land and gave Lot first pick of what he wanted. Seeing that the plains were well-watered, fertile and above all close at hand, Lot chose the best-looking terrain, leaving his uncle with the more remote wilderness of Canaan. They shook hands, wished each other well, and moved on to their new homes—Abraham to the hill country and Lot to the twin cities of Sodom and Gomorrah (13:10–12). But Lot made his decision without first checking out the cities to see what they were really like.

As cities, Sodom and Gomorrah were probably not on a par with New York, London or Paris, which offer culture and relative security to residents and tourists. Sodom was the capital city of perversion, where every deviant sexual practice was not only widely available but socially sanctioned.

JUDGMENT DAY

After Sodom and Gomorrah had set a new record for depravity, God scheduled the city for annihilation. When Abraham learned of this across-the-board indictment, he questioned the angel of the Lord who came to explore the area: "Will you sweep away the righteous with the wicked? What if there are 50 righteous people in the city? Will you really sweep it away and not spare the place for the sake of the 50 righteous people in it? Far be it from you to do such a thing—to kill the righteous with the wicked, treating the righteous and the wicked alike . . . Will not the Judge of all the earth do right?" (18:23–25)

Appreciating Abraham's passionate appeal, the Lord agreed to spare Sodom and Gomorrah if 50 righteous people could be found (18:26). Abraham continued to haggle with the Almighty, working from 50 people all the way down to ten. And for the sake of only ten, the Lord agreed to let the entire city live—but that was God's final offer (18:27–33). Abraham should have felt mightily relieved that he had bargained with the Lord and lived to tell the story. In any case, ten was the Lord's bottom line and not one less.

The angelic visitors asked: "Do you have anyone else here in Sodom who belongs to you? Get them out of here, because we are going to destroy this place. The outcry to the Lord against its people is so great that He has sent us to destroy it" (19:12–13).

When Lot informed his future sons-in-law of the disaster to come, they thought he was either kidding or out of his mind and ignored the alert. Lot was treated no differently than people today who claim to know the specific date for the end of the world.

As dawn approached, the angels pressed Lot to flee with his family to avoid being killed when the city was obliterated. They were led out of the city and sent on their way to safety, because not even ten righteous people could be found in Sodom and Gomorrah.

MRS. LOT

The angels specified that Lot's family needed to "flee to the mountains"—and not look back (19:17). Why were they told not to look back? It might have delayed their retreat to safety or caused them to be angry with God for what He had done. Or perhaps it would signify that they valued their home, friends, and community more than their relationship with the Lord. As they fled, Lot's wife did look back—and she was changed to a pillar of salt (19:26). The angels delayed the bombardment until Lot and his family could reach the small town of Zoar, out of harm's way. As the sun rose, super-heated sulphur rained down on Sodom and Gomorrah and the fertile plains around them, burning everything it touched (19:23–25).

After their escape Lot became a single parent of two headstrong young women who would create new family problems for generations to come. Although they had been saved from incineration, their sinful natures remained the same. Lot and the girls quickly left Zoar and moved to the mountains, where they they lived in a cave. This arrangement must have been challenging for young women accustomed to a higher standard of living than an extended camping trip in the wild. They were willing to do whatever it took to reclaim their former lives.

One day the older daughter said to the younger, "Our father is old, and there is no man around here to lie with us, as is the custom all over the earth. Let's get our father to drink wine and then lie with him and preserve our family line through our father" (19:31–32). So, that night the girls got Lot drunk, and the older daughter had relations with him while he slept. The next night the younger sister did the same, and both became pregnant by their father (19:33–36).

The girls had their babies—both sons. The older daughter named hers Moab, who grew to become the father of the Moabites. The younger daughter named her son Ben-ammi, and he became the father of the Ammonites (19:37–38). Throughout history both nations would be relentless enemies of Israel. If you thought the situation with Ishmael was bad, the ones involving Moab and Ben-ammi would be much worse. And it seemed like such a good idea at the time.

So, if an angel tells you to "Run, and don't look back!" do it—unless you want to end up like Mrs. Lot! She didn't even have time to ask if it was a good idea or not.

Seconds, Anyone?

Jacob and Esau

I saac, the successor to Abraham, remained childless into his old age, just as his father had been. As he hovered on the brink of becoming the next family patriarch, he knew he needed an heir in order to avert the same problem his parents had had with Hagar and Ishmael. "Isaac prayed to the Lord on behalf of his wife, because she was barren" (Gen. 25:21). To his credit, he sought the Lord's guidance before stumbling into trouble, not after he had already made a muddle of things. God abundantly answered his prayer and blessed Isaac and Rebekah with twin sons.

God explained to Rebekah, "Two nations are in your womb, and two peoples from within you will be separated; one people will be stronger than the other, and the older will serve the younger" (25:23). As if having twins wasn't complicated enough, this family had the makings of a bitter rivalry. The younger child would be honored and highly favored, while the older one would be his brother's servant—reversing the tradition of inheritance and the priority of the firstborn.

The twin boys could not have been more different. The firstborn had a ruddy complexion and lots of red hair, and he was called Esau, meaning "red." The second child came a moment later, grasping the back of his brother's foot. Isaac and Rebekah named their second son Jacob, meaning the "grasper" or "supplanter," which was fitting since he would displace his older sibling (25:25–26). Although separated at birth by mere seconds, the relationship between the brothers was distant and strained from the beginning, and it only got worse.

PLAYING FAVORITES

Esau became a skillful hunter and capable outdoorsman, providing extra meat for the family table—a handy son to have around. Jacob, on the other hand, "was a quiet man, staying among the tents" (25:27). One brother liked to be outside getting dirty, while the other enjoyed more refined pursuits. Perhaps on his birthday Esau received a bow and arrow and football equipment, while Jacob would have been more than pleased with an Easy-Bake oven and a gourmet cookbook.

Isaac, who liked the taste of fresh game, loved his son Esau more, while Rebekah favored Jacob, who spent much time at home with her. No doubt, both parents took sides whenever sibling rivalry erupted. In addition to playing favorites, Isaac and Rebekah loved their sons conditionally, based on what they could do, and more specifically, how they could help their mother and father. Consequently, rather than being best friends and playmates, Jacob and Esau were perpetual rivals, knowing that they were constantly being evaluated on their actions.

One day as Jacob was preparing lentil stew from a recipe in his new cookbook, Esau came in from hunting, hungry enough to eat anything in sight. That sounds like a typical teenage appetite.

"Little brother," Esau asked. "Can I have some of your stew? It smells delicious and I'm starving!"

BIRTHRIGHT AND BLESSING

Jacob's classic reaction would have been to whine or run away and complain to Rebekah. But this time he had something else in mind. "Sure, I can do that. First sell me your birthright" (25:31). The birthright involved special inheritance rights and privileges reserved for the first-born child, as well as the heir's position in the transference of tribal leadership. Although recognized as legal and binding, these rights could be transferred—but once transferred, there was no going back.

Esau replied with an exaggeration common to young people who think they are starving when in fact they are only slightly hungry: "Look, I am about to die . . . What good is the birthright to me?" (25:32). Jacob required Esau to swear to the transfer, no doubt having it signed, witnessed and notarized, which made it irrevocable.

Although Jacob may have played unfairly on Esau's vulnerability, Esau treated something sacred as having no value. In a family used to enabling self-doubt through constant comparisons of the twins, Esau's reaction is understandable. By that point, he didn't care—about family, God, inheritance, or his future. Jacob returned to his cooking knowing that he, the little brother, had won big-time! He had won, yes, but not without great cost.

Later Jacob and Rebekah conned an almost blind Isaac into giving the blessing, the part of the inheritance traditionally reserved for the first born, to Jacob. Now with both the birthright and the blessing, Jacob would inherit substantial wealth upon his father's demise. But what he really inherited was a shattered relationship with his parents and his brother. Instead of being best friends and eternal allies, they became perpetual enemies, with their descendants ready to kill or be killed across millennia right on through to today. I hope they both thought it was worth it, for that was one expensive bowl of stew that we're still paying for.

The Champ

Moses

⟋⟍⟋⟍

Genesis chronicles the story of humanity from Adam and Eve to Joseph—son of Jacob, heir to the covenant and the one who rescued the Hebrews from famine. The saga of the chosen people continues in the book of Exodus, as God delivers the Israelites out of bondage to form a new nation in the land of milk and honey.

Exodus includes the complete list of Jacob's sons, who formed the nucleus of the nation of Israel. Eventually "Joseph and all his brothers and all that generation died, but the Israelites were fruitful and multiplied greatly and became exceedingly numerous, so that the land was filled with them" (Exod. 1:1–7).

GROWING IN NUMBERS

They must have been fruitful indeed, growing from a total of 70 people when Joseph had all the relatives move to Egypt to escape the famine, until the Exodus 430 years later. Exodus 12:37 notes that when they left, there were "600,000 men on foot, besides women and children." A later reference, which cites contributions to the construction of the Tabernacle based on population, states that the number was 603,590 (38:26). Some estimates have placed the Hebrew population at the time of the Exodus in the millions, including women and children and those born along the way. At any rate, the Egyptians may have felt like a minority in their own country and thus seized control by using the Hebrews for free labor. The slaves needed a champion to lead them from bondage to freedom, and that man was Moses.

The story of Moses begins with Amram and Jochebed of the tribe of Levi (Levi was the son of Jacob and Leah, who founded one of the tribes of Israel). Amran and Jochebed married, and in due course had a son (2:1–2; 6:20). Amram lived to be 137 years old and had two other children—Aaron and Miriam.

Egyptian law at that time demanded that every male Hebrew baby be drowned in the Nile River. But when Jochebed held her infant son, she could not bring herself to kill him. Risking her own life by violating the edict, she hid him for the first three months of his life until she could no longer conceal his presence. Maybe the neighbors had heard the late night crying, or perhaps saw all the diapers hanging out on the clothesline.

Caught between the proverbial rock and a hard place, Jochebed designed an ingenious plan to obey the letter if not the intent of the law. This resourceful mother made a waterproof basket of papyrus reeds, covered with tar and pitch, to carry the child safely into the quiet water away from the current and the crocodiles.

RESCUE

Big sister Miriam secretly followed behind to make sure the tiny boat and precious crew sailed unimpeded to its intended destination—the same spot in the river where Pharaoh's daughter went to bathe each day. Exactly as planned, Pharaoh's daughter and her attendants came down to the river at the opportune time to "discover" the basket and the child. All the princess had to do was take one look at the little baby in the basket and there was no way she could toss him back into the river. When the baby cried her maternal instincts were stirred to action.

She probably knew that this child was a Hebrew baby because an Egyptian family would not have gone to such elaborate lengths to conceal and protect their child. He may have been wrapped in a distinctive cloth common only to the Hebrews, and she could not have missed the fact that he was circumcised, according to the covenant made between God and Abraham as a perpetual sign of that relationship (see Gen. 17 ff.).

Right on cue, Miriam popped up with a sensible solution to the problem of child care. She asked Pharaoh's daughter, "Shall I go and get one of the Hebrew women to nurse the baby for you?" and of course the reply was in the affirmative. Miriam just happened to know a lady who was perfectly capable of nursing a baby boy—his own mother, Jochebed. The princess asked Jochebed to nurse the child and paid her for doing so (2:4–9).

When the lad was older, perhaps a toddler, Jochebed brought her son back to the princess, who officially raised him as her own child. The Bible makes no mention of his name until he comes to live in the palace with the princess as the son of Egyptian royalty. Then he was given a name symbolic of his beginnings that meant, "I drew him out of the water"—Moses.

I wonder how the princess explained to her father, the Pharaoh, where this angelic olive-skinned baby boy came from? Did she refer to him as a gift from one of the Nile deities?

With no information on his formative years, the Bible jumps abruptly from Moses the baby to Moses the man, who has grown up in the best of both worlds. Scripture says that one day Moses left the friendly confines of the royal compound to see where his Hebrew relatives lived. He watched them as they worked under the cruel oppression of the Egyptian taskmasters, who treated them like beasts of burden. It must have been quite an eye-opener to see how the Hebrews dressed and how they were treated.

On that day of inspection and discovery of his ethnic heritage, Moses saw an Egyptian overseer beating a Hebrew slave. This appears to be the first time that Moses recognized the oppressed Israelites as his own countrymen. In his rage, he looked around to see if there were any witnesses. Seeing none, he killed the Egyptian and hastily buried the body in the sand. We are not told how he killed the overseer—with his bare hands, a sword, or a rock?—except that Moses thought he had escaped undetected (2:11–12).

ANTI-HERO?

Perhaps feeling morally superior to the taskmaster who got what he deserved, Moses went back out the next day to observe the Hebrews. He may have thought they would hail him as their protector. While out and about he saw two Hebrews fighting. Attempting to break up the altercation he asked one of them, "Why are you hitting your fellow Hebrew?" (2:13). But rather than seeing Moses as a great champion of the downtrodden the man fired back, "Who made you ruler and judge over us? Are you thinking of killing me as you killed the Egyptian?" (2:14).

Rather than the murder being a secret, it was now common knowledge. And if the slaves knew about it, Moses was sure the story would be the topic of conversation all across the kingdom.

When Pharaoh learned of the murder and the attempted cover-up, he tried to kill Moses. Perhaps, given the nature of infighting and power plays by royal families throughout history, this crisis might have provided an excellent opportunity to be rid of a potential rival. But before Pharaoh could track Moses down, he fled to Midian to hide and think things through (2:15). Moses never expected to leave the security and comfort of the palace to live as a fugitive, all for doing something he thought was a good idea at the time.

While Moses was in Midian, the Lord personally commissioned him to approach Pharaoh and persuade him to let the Hebrew slaves go. The Lord deflected each of Moses' attempts to decline this formidable job and assured him that his brother Aaron would be there to help him.

Moses returned to Egypt to confront his divinely appointed destiny and demanded that Pharaoh "Let the people go." He did—eventually, but only after a series of plagues ending with the death of every first-born in Egypt. When he saw how the mysterious death "passed over" the Hebrews, Pharaoh couldn't wait to let them go.

He quickly changed his mind, though, upon realizing that without slave labor his fellow Egyptians would have to build the treasure cities themselves. Pharaoh then ordered his charioteers to bring the slaves back by force. Underestimating the love of the Lord for His people, the Egyptian soldiers assumed the Hebrews were trapped between the Red Sea and their hard-charging chariots. As soon as God parted the Red Sea, the Hebrews crossed on dry land with the charioteers charging headlong after them. Pharaoh's men drowned in the middle of the sea after the Lord let the water rise again (Exod. 15:19).

After the charioteers disappeared beneath the foam, Miriam, once Moses' protector and prophetess, led the victory parade. She took a tambourine and led all the women in an impromptu celebration of Israel's deliverance from what had appeared to be certain death. "Sing to the Lord, for He is highly exalted. The horse and its rider He has hurled into the sea" (20–21). She must have celebrated her role in saving her little brother from death in the Nile, which ultimately made the exodus possible. She was probably proud of how Moses had turned out and must have smiled inwardly at her part in his success.

What About Us?

Aaron and Miriam

⟳⟲

Over time family pride evolved into envy and resentment as Moses took center stage while Miriam and Aaron were relegated to bit parts. Moses had a relationship with the Lord that the others could only imagine and wish for themselves. And in the case of Miriam and Aaron, sibling rivalry didn't get any easier to handle with the passing of time.

So rather than defend and support Moses, Miriam complained about her famous brother. Christian songwriter Keith Green sums up some of this rivalry and resentment in his song, "So You Wanna Go Back to Egypt?":

> *Moses acts like a big shot,*
> *Who does he think he is?*
> *It's true God does a lot of miracles*
> *But Moses thinks they're all his!*

WHISPERING

Miriam and Aaron started a derisive whispering campaign about Moses' wife, who was a Cushite from Midian and not a *proper* girl descended from Jacob and the patriarchs (Num. 12:1). You can almost hear the sarcasm dripping from each word. How many family squabbles over the years have been fought over someone's choice of a spouse?

Actually, Miriam's envy had nothing to do with her sister-in-law. She was upset because God spoke directly with and through Moses—not her. She and Aaron complained, "Has the Lord spoken only through Moses? Hasn't He also spoken through us?" (12:3).

In many cases growing older does not always guarantee maturity. Often, the aging process further accentuates our bad habits and character flaws. Part of that stems from resentment at seeing others advance while we stand still or fall behind. One of the surest signs of maturity is to shower praise and encouragement on someone who does something that you know you could do better. Thinking more highly of others than oneself is even harder when that person is a close relative or a famous sibling. World famous advice columnist Ann Landers has said, "The true measure of an individual is how he treats a person who can do him absolutely no good."

As Aaron and Miriam griped and whined, they forgot that the Lord heard every word, and He was not happy with their attack on His chosen deliverer. They thought they could just run their mouths with impunity since they were Moses' family. They could not have been more wrong.

Scripture says that the Lord spoke to the three of them—Moses, Aaron and Miriam—and commanded them to report to the tent of meeting on the double (12:4). This was not like when a mother calls her daughter in for supper or tells her it is time to turn off the TV and go to bed. Those commands usually have at least several follow-ups before we know she really means it. It was also far worse than hearing our name called over the PA system in front of the entire school and being ordered to report to the principal's office.

GOD'S VERDICT

Once the three siblings reached the tent of meeting, the Lord descended in visible presence in the form of a cloud-shaped column. There, He called them by name and told them to stand forward.

God said, "When a prophet of the Lord is among you, I reveal myself to him in visions, I speak to him in dreams. But this is not true of my servant Moses; he is faithful in all my house. With him I speak face to face, clearly and not in riddles; he sees the form of the Lord. Why then were you not afraid to speak against my servant Moses?" (12:6). It was as if the Lord was saying, "When I reveal Myself, I do so through the prophets and then through visions and dreams. But with Moses, I speak directly. How dare you criticize this man? Did you really think I wouldn't notice or care? Wrong!"

The Lord's anger "burned against them, and He left them" (12:9). Did Aaron and Miriam feel a profound sense of dread? Did they wonder if their futures would be short-lived?

They did not have long to wait for the Lord's verdict, for as the cloud lifted, Aaron turned to his sister and saw that her skin was white and flaky, like snow—she had leprosy. One moment before she was clean, normal and the picture of health. Now she was infected with a full-blown case of the most terrifying disease of the day (12:10).

Aaron pleaded with Moses not to hold their sin against them. He and Miriam confessed their arrogance and begged Moses to intercede with God on their behalf to heal Miriam. Moses did as he was asked. He did not repay evil for evil or attempt to get even in any way.

The Lord replied that if Miriam had been spat upon, she would have been ceremonially defiled and then confined in disgrace for seven days outside the camp (12:14). Seven days was time enough for everyone to reflect on what had happened, to learn a valuable lesson in obedience and loyalty, and unfortunately, to delay the already anxious travelers in their journey to Canaan.

At the end of her punishment, Miriam was restored to health and to the fellowship of the Israelite camp. I wonder if she had to endure cold stares from her travel mates for a time. We may never know. But we can reasonably imagine that she never chose to speak ill of brother Moses again.

"Let's Make an Idol"

Aaron

⤳⟨◉⟩⤳

A aron made his own bad decision with greater consequences than Miriam's, for it affected him, his family and thousands of his countrymen.

On the way to the Promised Land, when the huge caravan of refugees from the Egyptian brick pits stopped at Mt. Sinai, the Lord took Moses up the mountain with Him for 40 days. There He prepared him for leadership and gave him the Law—what we know today as the Ten Commandments. When the Lord finished speaking to Moses, He gave him the commandments on two stone tablets, engraved by the finger of God.

Meanwhile, back at the camp, the natives were getting restless. They didn't know if Moses was dead or alive, and could not investigate, since God had ordered no one to touch the base of the mountain under penalty of death. After seeing how the Lord had treated the first born of Egypt and the charioteers, that was a gamble no one wanted to take just to satisfy their curiosity.

TERRIFIED SHEEP

Without the visible presence of Moses to guide them, the Hebrews lost their trust in the God who had freed and saved them several times before. As long as Moses personally led them and took responsibility for handling the Lord's demands, things were tolerable. But without that direct, tangible leadership that required little faith, they were like a panic-stricken flock of aimless, terrified sheep.

When it seemed that Moses was never coming back down from the mountain, the people gathered around Aaron and said, "Come, make us gods who will go before us. As for this fellow Moses who brought us up out of Egypt, we don't know what has happened to him" (Exod. 32:1). They called Moses "this fellow"—how soon they forgot all he had done for them! Even Aaron may have begun thinking of Moses in the past tense.

Aaron could have reminded everyone of the Lord's blessings and of how Moses had fought for their release from Pharaoh. He could have encouraged them to believe in the Lord who works in ways too majestic for them to understand. He could have done a great many things, but he didn't.

With no time for reflection, almost in the next breath, Aaron answered, "Take off the gold earrings that your wives, your sons and your daughters are wearing, and bring them to me" (32:2). Then he melted them down and cast an idol in the shape of a calf. When the idol was finished he presented it to the assembly and declared, "These are your gods, O Israel, who brought you up out of Egypt" (32:4).

THE STYLIZED BOVINE

By then Moses had received the first commandment establishing the priority of worship. God would never share His people or His majesty with anything made by humankind. But while Moses was off receiving the law, his own brother was down in the camp making a golden calf to worship and building an altar in front of it, proclaiming, "Tomorrow there will be a festival to the Lord" (32:6).

Aaron really had his priorities wrong, for when he said "there will be a festival to the Lord," most Bible translations show the name of God as LORD (all CAPS), meaning the Lord Almighty, Jehovah, the One Moses was at that moment meeting with on the mountain, the one who is holy, pure, powerful, perfect and "other"—unlike anything or anyone in the entire universe. Aaron was mistaking the "Creator, Preserver and Governor of all things," for a scale model of a stylized bovine whose only claim to power was the value of the gold and what it could buy. Bright and early the next morning, the people brought sacrifices. With that act they did more than just set aside meat from slain animals or other offerings. They made an overt declaration that the idol was worthy of their time, their devotion and their prayer by bestowing "worth-ship" on it rather than on God.

The people indulged in some serious feasting and revelry like there was no tomorrow. For some that was indeed true, for as they were singing, dancing and drinking themselves into a stupor, the Lord told Moses, "Go down, because your people, whom you brought up out of Egypt, have become corrupt. They have been quick to turn away from what I commanded them and have made themselves an idol cast in the shape of a calf. They have bowed down to it and sacrificed to it and have said, 'These are your gods, O Israel, who brought you up out of Egypt.' I have seen these people," the Lord said to Moses, "and they are a stiff-necked people. Now leave me alone so that my anger may burn against them and that I may destroy them. Then I will make you into a great nation" (32:7–10).

It is interesting that the Lord referred to the Israelites as Moses' people—not His own. But that is accurate since they had forgotten both the Lord's provision and how to worship Him. They had forgotten the most fundamental part of their covenant relationship with God since the days of Abraham, Isaac and Jacob, which required them to obey, worship and show gratitude to God.

MOSES INTERCEDES

The opportunity to be remembered as the "father of many nations," in the manner of Abraham could have been a heady appeal to Moses' ego and desire for achievement. Yet Moses came to Israel's defense and interceded again on behalf of the Hebrews. "Lord," he said, "why should your anger burn against your people, whom you brought out of Egypt with great power and a mighty hand? Why should the Egyptians say, 'It was with evil intent that He brought them out, to kill them in the mountains and to wipe them off the face of the earth'? Turn from your fierce anger; relent and do not bring disaster on your people. Remember your servants Abraham, Isaac and Israel, to whom you swore by your own self: 'I will make your descendants as numerous as the stars in the sky and I will give your descendants all this land I promised them, and it will be their inheritance forever'" (32:11–13).

Responding to Moses' passionate concern, the Lord chose to spare the people's lives. God told Moses to go back down the mountain with the Ten Commandments and return to the camp to confront the evil that Aaron had set loose. On the way he met Joshua, who thought all the shouting was the sound of war, but Moses heard singing and celebrating instead—not singing of praise and worship to the Lord but wild frenzy like a Mardi Gras run amok (see 32:15–18).

When he finally reached the camp and saw the debauchery for himself, Moses grew furious with Aaron and everyone else. He took the two precious stone tablets, threw them to the ground and smashed them to pieces. After a substantial tongue lashing reminding the Hebrews of their rights and responsibilities as the people of God, Moses took the golden calf, ground it into fine gold powder, mixed it with the drinking water and made the people drink it. Although the gold would never be dissolved and would remain intact as fine powder, no one wanted the disagreeable task of trying to recover the gold dust from the camp latrines (32:19–20).

Moses grabbed his wayward brother and demanded, "What did these people do to you, that you led them into such great sin?" Immediately Aaron attempted to make excuses, deflecting blame and responsibility. The people had *forced* him to make the idol, he insisted.

"Do not be angry," Aaron answered. "You know how prone these people are to evil. They said to me, 'Make us gods who will go before us. As for this fellow Moses who brought us up out of Egypt, we don't know what has happened to him.' So I told them, 'Whoever has any gold jewelry, take it off.' Then they gave me the gold, and I threw it into the fire, and out came this calf!" (22–24). Yeah right, Aaron! The gold went into the fire and the idol popped out all by itself. Did he really think Moses would buy that one? Did he think God would overlook that bit of ludicrous rationalization? Aaron could not deny saying that "these are your gods who brought you out of Egypt," since there were numerous witnesses around.

Moses looked around and saw the people running wild, thanks in large part to his brother's lack of leadership. He knew that Israel's enemies might have considered the Lord and His people nothing more than a joke. To bring the situation back under control, he rallied the Levites and instructed them to carry out divine judgment and punishment.

He said to them, "This is what the Lord, the God of Israel, says: 'Each man strap a sword to his side. Go back and forth through the camp from one end to the other, each killing his brother and friend and neighbor.'" About 3,000 people died (27–28).

Moses thanked the Levites who were set apart that day for the Lord's service. In the future they would serve God in the Tabernacle and Temple, and they would be the only tribe of Israel not to receive property as their portion of Israel's inheritance. The following day, after the survivors had a chance to contemplate the enormity of their transgression, Moses met with them again. He said, "You have committed a great sin. But now I will go up to the Lord; perhaps I can make atonement for your sin" (29–30). He interceded on their behalf once again—for the same ones who had disobeyed, complained and rejected the Lord. Moses told God that he would rather have his name blotted out of the Lord's book than continue his life and ministry without family and friends.

THE PLAGUE

The Lord said that when the right time came, He would do the reckoning and would punish those who deserved to be punished. In the meantime, Moses was told to get the caravan back on track to Canaan without further delay (31–34). To make sure He had everyone's complete and undivided attention, the Lord sent a plague. It certainly must have made an impression.

Because the Lord takes His relationship with His people so seriously, He told Moses to "Leave this place, you and the people you brought up out of Egypt, and go up to the land I promised on oath to Abraham, Isaac and Jacob, saying, 'I will give it to your descendants.' I will send an angel before you and drive out the Canaanites, Amorites, Hittites, Perizzites, Hivites and Jebusites. Go up to the land flowing with milk and honey. But I will not go with you, because you are a stiff-necked people and I might destroy you on the way . . . Now take off your ornaments and I will decide what to do with you'" (33:1–5).

Finally, the former slaves were on their way again—with the promise that the Lord would protect them against their enemies on the way to Canaan. When the Hebrews heard that promise, they stripped off their ornaments in mourning and deep respect, because God had chosen not to lead them personally lest He become angry enough to turn them into ashes. They would have to rely on Moses to show them the way.

Aaron's sin compounded the peoples' sin so that thousands paid with their lives, and the trip to the Promised Land was further delayed. I am sure they all thought it was a good idea at the time.

Tongue-Tied

Moses

చిళిఖిఖ

Moses made another poor decision that, on the surface, seemed much less significant than his murder of the Egyptian taskmaster. But a lapse of trust and an uncontrollable burst of temper cost him his chance to enter the Promised Land and bring his divine mission to conclusion.

Imagine the perpetual frustration Moses must have felt while being responsible for more than 600,000 complaining, ungrateful ex-slaves. They should have been thrilled to be free and going home, but instead they griped about everything—food, water, weather, heat, cold—and especially Moses' leadership. Many of the more vocal ones even wanted to return to the brick pits in Egypt rather than submit to the Lord's authority working through Moses. Nothing Moses did was right, and none of his efforts were appreciated in the least. "Moses, the Danites are letting their sheep run through the Asherite camp again"; "MOSES, ARE WE THERE YET!"

UNHAPPY CAMPERS

On their way out of bondage to Caanan, the entire company set out from the Desert of Sin, traveling from place to place as the Lord led them. When they camped at Sephardim, there was no water for the people to drink (Exod. 17:1). Since there is only so much water a person can carry without canteens or a tanker truck, the Israelites soon began to complain of an extraordinary thirst.

Moses grew more than a little irked by their reaction and demands, for after all, the Lord had never failed to sustain them in every way before. Why would God let them die of thirst after all the effort He had expended to convince Pharaoh to let them leave Egypt in the first place?

Scripture says that the people grumbled against Moses in an undercurrent of discontent that rumbled throughout the camp (17:2–3). "Give us water to drink," they demanded. "Why did you bring us up out of Egypt to make us and our children and livestock die of thirst?" By this point Moses was really angry. "He cried out to the Lord," the Scripture says. "What am I to do with these people? They are almost ready to stone me" (17:4).

Always as patient as He is holy, the Lord instructed Moses to walk on a bit with a few of the elders to a large rock in Horeb. There he was to take his shepherd's staff and strike the rock and there would be water enough for all. Moses obeyed, gave the rock a good whack, and just as the Lord had promised, out gushed plenty of water. And for the moment, everyone was happy with God and Moses. Things would change in a hurry with this bunch.

You would think that the people would learn to trust God for their practical as well as spiritual needs. But since they were as demanding and forgetful as we are, you would be wrong. Further down the trail the water supply ran low and the people bellyached again. "Why did you bring the Lord's community into this desert, that we and our livestock should die here? Why did you bring us up out of Egypt to this terrible place? It has no grain or figs, grapevines or pomegranates. And there is no water to drink!" (Num. 20:4–5).

Again Moses presented their concerns to the Lord and sought His guidance. This time Moses was to take Aaron and speak to the rock in front of the people, and it would provide water enough for all. And for the first time since he had been called to deliver Israel out of Egypt, he disobeyed the Lord.

Everyone could feel the heat of Moses' anger. We might try to understand Moses' displeasure and attribute it to blowing off steam at the aggravation he had to endure. Moses and Aaron gathered the people together in front of the rock and Moses said to them, "Listen, you rebels. Must we bring you water out of this rock?" (20:10).

GOING HIS OWN WAY

Moses didn't speak to the rock, as ordered, or just give it a tap; he gave it two solid resounding shots worthy of a Babe Ruth home run blast. As before, water spurted from the rock and everyone was happy again—everyone but the Lord.

Far from giving Moses a pass on this one, the Lord said to Moses, "Because you did not trust in me enough to honor me as holy in the sight of the Israelites, you will not bring this community into the land I give them" (20:12). Moses, in effect, had treated God with disrespect, which couldn't be done without considerable risk or severe penalty.

Many years later the prophet Malachi echoed a similar sentiment—that the people had despised the Lord's name by showing great contempt. "A son honors his father, and a servant his master. If I am a father, where is the honor due me? If I am a master, where is the respect due me?" says the Lord Almighty. "It is you, O priests, who show contempt for my name. But you ask, 'How have we shown contempt for your name?' God says, 'You despise my name'" (Mal. 1:6–12).

The word "despise" in Hebrew has a negative connotation that does not translate easily into English. In Hebrew, despise means not malevolent contempt but the holding of someone in such low regard that they are considered almost worthless. Through Malachi God said that the priests treated their relationship with God this way because they did not honor His name and His altar with their sacrifices.

For a sacrifice to be acceptable, animals had to be clean, without disease or defect. Malachi indicates that the animals of his day were diseased, maimed and possibly even stolen. God viewed them as unclean because they cost the giver nothing. It is no sacrifice to give what would have otherwise gone out with the trash. Do we do the same with our service and worship to God? Did Moses?

The people wanted their immediate desires met, while God wanted them to trust Him to provide for their deepest needs. The Lord began the Ten Commandments by stating that He was to be their God with no other rival, and to keep His day and His name holy. But Moses had shifted the focus to himself instead of trusting in the perfect promises of God. The people had held the Lord in contempt because all they wanted was water, not a relationship with the One who provided water and everything else.

FROM A DISTANCE

Moses did an admirable job leading the mob of ex-slaves out of bondage, interceding on their behalf with the Lord and paving the way for them to become a nation. The Israelites would never know how close they had come to extermination had it not been for Moses' personal relationship with the Lord. But since his lack of trust made God appear helpless and worthless, God would only allow him to see the Promised Land from the top of Mt. Nebo. Despite all he had done for the Israelites, Moses could not see his life's work through to completion because he had treated the Lord disrespectfully in front of many witnesses.

"Moses climbed Mount Nebo from the plains of Moab to the top of Pisgah, across from Jericho. There the Lord showed him the whole land—from Gilead to Dan, all of Naphtali, the territory of Ephraim and Manasseh, all the land of Judah as far as the western sea, the Negev and the whole region from the Valley of Jericho, the City of Palms, as far as Zoar. Then the Lord said to him, 'this is the land I promised on oath to Abraham, Isaac and Jacob when I said, "I will give it to your descendants." I have let you see it with your eyes, but you will not cross over into it.' And Moses the servant of the Lord died there in Moab, as the Lord had said" (Deut: 1–5).

What a terrible price to pay for impatience, frustration and a bad decision. He made it so close, all the way from Egypt to a view of home in the distance. Close, but yet so far away.

Hot Stuff, For Real?

Nadab and Abihu

C hildren often resemble human video recorders, internalizing everything their parents say and do. Parents, of course, would like their
kids to know them as paragons of wisdom and to follow their sagacious
precepts so that life will be simple, neat and trouble-free. Yet far more
often, kids are privy to prejudices, impatience, flashes of temper, character compromises and other less than virtuous acts. If they truly were
recording everything, it would be prudent to review the tapes periodi-
cally, edit out the questionable parts and enhance the good ones. Sadly,
that is not possible. Often our children remember precisely what we
want them to forget and perpetuate these ills for generations to come.
Such was the case with Nadab and Abihu, who learned lessons of disobedience and compromise from their father and role model for ministry—Aaron.

After the Golden Calf incident, the Lord decided that the tribe of Levi,
to which Moses and Aaron belonged, would have no ancestral land
holdings. Instead, the Levites would be priests who would serve in the
Tabernacle and later in the Temple in Jerusalem. One old adage says,
"Hold your friends close—hold your enemies even closer." Perhaps the
Lord wanted Aaron and his family close by where He could keep a sharp
eye on them in order to prevent another debacle like the Golden Calf.

Ignorance comes from not knowing what is expected. Folly, however,
is a learned behavior that stems from choosing the wrong over the right.
It may be the result of making wrong assumptions and conclusions
about what we have learned. But then again, arrogance might be at the

heart of the problem. So we may ask, were Nadab and Abihu arrogant or foolish? The answer would have to be yes—for both.

LAWS

In the book of Leviticus, the Lord unveils a plan for acceptable worship with all of the requirements, observances and awe necessary for a holy God to live in close proximity with His extraordinarily flawed people. Leviticus identifies all of the dietary laws, the process of offering sacrifices, which items are acceptable sacrifices and which are not. Scripture prescribes carefully detailed ways to prepare, kill, and offer the sacrifice. Everything had to be done correctly with reverence and deep, heart-felt respect. Some sacrifices were to be completely burned while others could be used as food for the priests and their families.

The Lord commanded Moses: "Bring Aaron and his sons, their garments, the anointing oil, the bull for the sin offering, the two rams and the basket containing bread made without yeast and gather the entire assembly at the entrance to the Tent of Meeting" (Lev. 8:1–3).

Moses summoned Aaron and his sons and washed them with water prior to a complex ordination service that included new clothes, consecrated utensils and special recognition of their priestly responsibilities. Moses also clarified the meaning and purpose of the sacrifice system. Sacrifices were not to forgive sins but rather to cover them by an offering of the blameless for the guilty, and to show just how needy and evil people were, compared to the holy, perfect nature of God (8:4–9:6).

SACRIFICES

Sacrifices were nothing new to that part of the world, since every country offered sacrifices of some sort to their deities. What is significant is that people took on the character of the deity worshipped. If a deity involved ritual prostitution, for example, a worshipper could not be chaste or celibate. If a god was violent, like Ares, the Greek god of war, it was impossible to be a pacifist. Our Lord needed to train and prepare His people to be holy. Nothing less than reverential awe would do. Nothing less than complete obedience would be accepted, and certainly not something done with arrogance, presumption or frivolous lack of commitment.

In our culture we have a skewed image of holiness. We think of darkened cathedrals, solemn music, gaunt monks chanting songs to a God who is far removed from us, incomprehensible and unapproachable— certainly not One who exists in the rough and tumble world of families, work, business and recreation. In Hebrew, though, the word for holy is *kabed*, which means heavy. In its initial application, this word had no direct connection to God. But over time it has come to denote the solemnity and majesty of God, conveying that He is not one to be trifled with, taken for granted or in any way accommodated.

Moses, Aaron and the other priests were commanded to remain near the front of the Tent of Meeting for seven days of sacrifice and preparation before their ordination. They needed to be ready to serve mentally, physically and above all, spiritually as God's representatives in worship. None of this was to be entered into lightly, and failure to carry out these instructions carried fatal consequences. "Do not leave the entrance to the Tent of Meeting for seven days, until the days of your ordination are completed, for your ordination will last seven days. What has been done today has been commanded by the Lord to make atonement for you. You must stay at the entrance to the Tent of Meeting day and night for seven days and do what the Lord requires, *so you will not die*; for that is what I have been commanded" (8:33–35). What part of "so you will not die" didn't they understand?

NO SHORT CUTS

On the eighth day Moses called for Aaron, his sons and the elders of Israel to begin atoning for the sins of the priests before they were ordained and commissioned. In Leviticus 9 the Lord specifies the type of offering and how it is to be presented. There were to be no short cuts or half measures, because the first offerings were for the priests' sins. Only when those offerings were accepted were they allowed to offer sacrifices for the sins of Israel. Note that these sins were ones committed by accident or ignorance—not with malice, premeditation or disregard for the Lord's commands. In Hebrew more serious offenses are referred to as "sins with a high hand." Jesus Christ is both the offering for our sins and the perfect High Priest—who deals with not only the sins we commit but the sin nature that corrupts even our best intentions. Without sin of His own to be atoned for, He was able to pay the full price and penalty for sin so that we, the guilty, could go free.

Moses reminded them, "This is what the Lord has commanded you to do, so that the glory of the Lord may appear to you" (9:6). Aaron and his sons offered the sacrifices exactly as the book of Leviticus dictated from beginning to end (9:7–21).

Then Aaron lifted his hands toward the people and blessed them. After having sacrificed the sin offering, the burnt offering and the fellowship offering, he stepped down. He and Moses entered the Tent of Meeting, and when they reappeared and blessed the people again the glory of the Lord shone. Fire emanated from His presence and totally consumed the burnt offering, incinerating all of the meat, bones and fat portions on the altar. When the people saw it, they shouted for joy and fell prostrate before the Lord (9:22–24). Moses and Aaron prayed and fire consumed the offering—no gas jets, no matches, nothing theatrical—only the holiness of the Lord Almighty.

COCKINESS

After the fire fell from the Lord indicating his acceptance of the offering, the people were filled with awe. Chapter 10 goes on to reveal how Aaron's sons, Nadab and Abihu "took their censers, put fire in them and added incense; and they offered unauthorized fire before the Lord, contrary to His command" (10:1). They just didn't get it.

Immediately, "fire came out from the presence of the Lord and consumed them, and they died before the Lord" (10:2). They didn't have the opportunity to learn from their mistake, because it was not really a mistake. Theirs was a sin of arrogant presumption. At first glance we might think the Lord was a bit hasty in His execution of judgment. Yet Nadab and Abihu, who had been through the ordination process and knew the right thing to do, were not the right people to do it.

There was no awe, no reverence, and no wonder. They did not have the right fire, the right attitude or the right heart of service. Because of all this, *they* became the burnt offering instead of some unlucky animal. They figured fire is fire and what difference does it make. The difference is that it made God look bad. Do that at your peril, especially when the

Lord is setting up a new nation founded on worship of "the Creator, Preserver and Governor of all things, and who is the only proper object of religious worship" (Salvation Army Doctrine #2).

To Nabab and Abihu, worship of the Lord was not of paramount significance. Boy, did they ever learn that lesson the hard way. For all the ceremony they had just experienced, they were unreachable and unteachable. So, rather than have these two rotten apples spoil the barrel for the rest of Israel, the Lord took them out. In fact, their crime was so serious that the Lord forbade Israel to mourn for them. The brothers were unceremoniously taken outside the camp and quickly buried in the Valley of Achor (which means valley of trouble in Hebrew) somewhere near Jericho.

God in His great mercy would later redeem this site as the "door of hope" in eighth century B.C. Just before Assyria invaded and conquered the Northern Kingdom, The Lord reached out to the Israelites one last time to repent of their sins (Hosea 2:15).

The lesson for us is that although God is love, He is not one to be taken lightly. We can never forget that He is God and not One to be treated with disrespect, arrogance, or lack of reverence—ever.

Stopping for Souvenirs
Achan

ᘓᕣᕕᕗ

It is amazing how sins have a habit of coming back to haunt us, even when we cover our tracks and leave no witnesses. Our sins have no fibers, hair, blood, DNA or fingerprints, but they still have a way of making our lives miserable until God deals with them.

On the way to the Promised Land the Israelites were ordered to defeat the fortified city of Jericho. Since the entire city was to be an offering to God, no one was allowed to take any souvenirs. God wanted to help the people remember to trust Him to take care of their needs and to obey His commands. The Hebrews could not afford to lose either their trust or obedience and still hope to live in right relationship with God. They all knew better, or at least they should have.

A ROUT

The Bible tells us that Jericho fell just as God had promised (Josh. 6). But a short time later, Joshua sent a small detachment to fight the city of Ai and the Israelites were defeated. They should have been able to overtake the entire city with little or no effort—"with one hand tied behind their back." That was not the case. When the Israelite army went into battle, they were routed and took heavy casualties for the first time. Until then they had been blessed with a not too secret, ultimate weapon—the Lord God Jehovah (7:1–6).

Joshua and the elders of the tribes fell prostrate before God, begging to know why the battle had gone so poorly. They believed that the cause for defeat was a spiritual failure rather than a military one.

"Lord, what is happening?" Joshua cried. "Why did you leave us? If this was going to happen, it would have been best that you had left us back where we were on the other side of the Jordan and not started this campaign in the first place."

The Lord told Joshua that one of the Israelites had flagrantly disobeyed Him by looting forbidden goods from Jericho. This sin had to be confronted before God would help them again. So Joshua ordered all the people to assemble, and by lot he chose the tribe of Judah. From that tribe, he selected the clan of the Zerahites, the family of Zimri and finally, Achan. Joshua singled him out from the entire population of hundreds of thousands of people—talk about finding a needle in a haystack!

"My son," Joshua ordered. "Give glory to the Lord, the God of Israel, and give Him the praise. Tell me what you have done; do not hide it from me" (7:19). "I did it," Achan admitted. "I have sinned against God. When I saw a beautiful robe from Babylon and big chunks of silver and gold I went crazy. I knew it was wrong, but it was more wealth than I had ever seen, right there for the taking. So I took it and buried it under my tent, and it is there right now."

From I Chronicles 2:7 we learn that Achan belonged to a prominent family in Judah, so in all likelihood he was not motivated by need. Was he greedy or just plain cheap? Was he looking for some nice souvenirs for the wife and kids to remind them of their trip to Jericho? Or did lust and avarice tempt him to run the risk of being caught and bringing harm to himself and family? Whatever it was, Achan did not listen and was now in deep trouble.

A quick search revealed the loot right where Achan said it was.

"Why have you brought this disaster on us, Achan?" Joshua asked. "Why did you do this thing when you knew it was wrong?"

READING HIS FACE

How did Joshua know what Achan had done? How did the others know? Maybe the song by the Eagles is truer than we imagine.

You can't hide your lyin' eyes,
And your smile is a thin disguise,
Thought by now you'd realize,
There ain't no way to hide your lyin' eyes.

As a result of his defiance, Achan and his entire family were stoned to death. Then all their possessions were cremated and buried as a permanent reminder of the danger of disobedience.

Because nothing happened right away, Achan thought he had gotten away with it. But sin always has a way of coming back to trip us up. The result might not always be this dramatic, but lies, deceptions and "small" sins corrupt our best efforts and damage the harmony of a close relationship with God.

Numbers 32:23 is just as true for us as for the ancients: "You may be sure that your sin will find you out." Before a God who knows our hearts we can't hide our lyin' eyes. But we can praise God that I John 1:9 is also true: "If we confess our sins, He [God] is faithful and just and will forgive us our sins and purify us from all unrighteousness."

It was a shame that Achan had to learn that lesson the hard way.

"Oh, My Aching Head!"

General Sisera

⌘⌒⌒⌒

The Lord never uses the world's standards when He recruits people to do exceptional things for Him. While the world selects persons with great skill, God desires those who have willing hearts. Some of those willing—His most unusual warriors—are recorded in the book of Judges. Israel had finally moved into the Promised Land, most of the great leaders had died, and the country had no king to unite behind. In terms of ethical behavior, everyone pretty much relied on their own discretion, often with disastrous consequences.

The people of Israel knew what God required of them, even though they never quite seemed to get with the program. God wanted them to worship Him in holiness and truth and to trust in His provision. Hebrew history abounded with knowledge of God's care—He had rescued them from 430 years of bondage in Egypt, guided them through 40 years of wandering in the desert, and finally, brought them safely to their homeland and inheritance. All they had to do in return was possess the land by completely driving out the Canaanite tribes who lived there. They seemed able to manage that as long as Israel had a great leader empowered by God, like Joshua. But without his excellent brand of leadership, they were in serious trouble.

Joshua, Israel's general and successor to Moses, summoned the people to Shechem for a solemn convocation before they separated and headed to their respective homes in the land of Canaan. Seeking to ensure that the people truly honored the Lord's expectations, he reminded them of what God had done for them over the years (Josh. 24:1–12).

JOSHUA'S WARNING

Joshua warned that God would not tolerate sharing the Israelites' hearts in the worship of pagan fertility gods. Neither would He overlook the breaking of solemn vows of spiritual fidelity. If the Israelites broke their promises, God would be as stern in His punishment as He had been compassionate in His care.

The people pledged to love and serve God alone as they returned home to claim their inheritance. They managed to do this fairly well throughout Joshua's lifetime. But after he died at the age of 110, new generations, who did not recall his influence or know firsthand of the Lord's provision, became as wicked as the pagans they were to have driven out. "The Israelites did evil in the eyes of the Lord. They provoked the Lord to anger because they forsook Him and served Baal and the Ashtoreths. In His anger against Israel, the Lord handed them over to raiders who plundered them. He sold them to their enemies all around, whom they were no longer able to resist" (2:11–14).

The people forgot the things of God, willingly "prostituted themselves" to other gods and pagan practices, and evoked the righteous anger of God. After the values of the Israelites had rotted from within, marauders from the surrounding nations took whatever they wanted, whenever they wanted it.

Invasion and oppression spurred the people to beg for the Lord's intervention during a dangerous era. Because of the Lord's great compassion for His people, whose only claim to redress was His own unchanging covenant with them, God sent special judges to carry out justice, lead military campaigns, and eliminate idolatrous settings. Unfortunately, though, as soon as a crisis passed or a judge died, the people quickly slid back into their familiar pattern, creating a continuing cycle of rebellion, apostasy, prayer, repentance and deliverance (2:18).

One of the chief oppressors was Jabin, a king of Canaan, who, along with his general-in-chief, Sisera, terrorized Israel for 20 years with a huge army and 900 charioteers. Going into battle against those iron chariots with bladed hubcaps must have been the ancient equivalent of trying to stop tanks with rocks (4:2–3).

DEBORAH

The Lord sent Deborah, a married prophetess who was already dispensing justice, to resolve the latest crisis facing the Israelites. Deborah, a remarkable leader in a patriarchal society, had been holding court near the towns of Ramah and Bethel in the hill country of Ephraim (4:4–5). Informed of the Lord's plan to defeat the Canaanite armies by prophetic revelation, she summoned Barak, one of Israel's trusted military leaders. She instructed him to take 10,000 warriors to Mount Tabor, where the Lord would deliver Jabin and Sisera's army and all their chariots into Israel's hands.

Barak must have felt dread, fear or just sought to cover all the bases, for he stipulated, "If you go with me, I will go; but if you don't go with me, I won't go" (4:8). So Deborah agreed to accompany Barak and the army, but she indicated that the honor for winning the day would go to a nomadic housewife, a "tent-wife" named Jael. Jael, who was married to Heber the Kenite, a descendant of Moses' family, happened to be passing through the vicinity of Mount Tabor as Sisera's army was massing to counter Barak's mobilization. Heber's encampment was no coincidence; it was God's hand liberating Israel (4:9).

Although Sisera started out smugly confident of his army's military prowess, the battle soon became a rout and Jabin's army was slaughtered. Seeing that all was lost, Sisera abandoned his troops and fled as fast as his feet could carry him.

Frantically running for his life, he stopped to take a breather at Jael's tent, feeling reasonably safe since the king of Hazor and the Kenites were on friendly terms. Jael went out to meet Sisera and invited him into her tent, offering him sanctuary and rest. She covered him with a blanket, let him relax and lulled him into a false sense of security. It was just like the well-known verse of the fly being offered the comfort of the parlor—by the hungry spider!

A PERMANENT NAP

"I'm thirsty," he said. "Please give me some water." But instead of water she gave him milk, and everyone knows the formula for sleep: exertion + warm milk = sound sleep. Unfortunately for General Sisera, his nap would be permanent.

Scripture says that "Jael, Heber's wife, picked up a tent peg and a hammer and went quietly to him while he [Sisera] lay fast asleep, exhausted. She drove the peg through his temple into the ground, and he died."

When Barak and his men arrived in pursuit of Sisera, Jael went out to meet them and showed them that he had been securely nailed to the ground. And from that day the Israelites grew more and more powerful until they were finally rid of Jabin the Canaanite king (4:19–24).

This story may seem strangely out of character for God, who blesses the meek and honors the peacemakers. Yet life was violent then, as a new nation was being forged in a lawless, immoral and brutal land. These were the labor pains of a theocracy like nothing the world had seen before.

Because God used such an odd weapon and an unusual champion—a tent-wife with some warm milk, common sense, bravery and a powerful mallet—there could be no doubt that He was the true Deliverer. If the Lord can achieve His ends with a faithful woman and a tent peg, imagine what He could do with us—if we let Him. And if someone offers you a glass of warm milk and a little snooze while you are running for your life—don't stop! Keep on running!

The Tourist Attraction

Gideon

A decision that on first consideration may seem logical and safe often causes nothing but grief as the situation explodes into catastrophe. Such was the case for Gideon and for Israel.

Fresh from their victory over the army of Midian with only 300 soldiers, (Judg. 6:1–7:23 *ff.*), Gideon, another one of Israel's judges, and his soldiers chased the stragglers all the way back to the Midian border. There they captured the Midianite leaders, Oreb and Zeeb, who were summarily executed. No sooner had Gideon returned to civilian life than the people of Israel wanted to make him king. "Rule over us—you, your son and your grandson—because you have saved us out of the hand of Midian" (8:22). They forgot that Gideon was only an instrument of God's miraculous deliverance, for the Lord could have used anyone, regardless of age or experience, to lead Israel. Fortunately, Gideon did not submit to the lure of ambition and told them, "I will not rule over you, nor will my son rule over you. The Lord will rule over you" (8:23).

Way to go Gideon! He had his priorities straight and gave honor and praise to Almighty God, where it rightfully belonged. He did everything perfectly—well, almost—for practically with his next breath he opened the door to idolatry, undermining the effectiveness of his previous efforts.

CHIPPING IN

"I do have one request, that each of you give me an earring from your share of the plunder." (It was the custom of the Canaanite tribes to wear gold earrings).

In full agreement with the project to fund a kind of war memorial, each man chipped in a ring from his share of the spoils. The weight of the rings came to 1,700 shekels—680 ounces of solid gold, not counting the other ornaments, pendants, royal robes and decorative chains the Midianites had on their camels' necks (8:24–26).

Rather than make a simple plaque for posterity to remember the battle, Gideon took the gold and designed an ephod—similar to an armor breastplate—to commemorate the victory over Midian. He kept it on display in his hometown where it became a major tourist attraction. Perhaps people took a detour on their summer vacations to go see Gideon's ephod—just down the road from the alligator wrestlers and the world's largest ball of string. Visitors to the site could remember the Lord's power in battle when they saw this symbol of divine protection.

Bad choice. Gideon should have asked God what He wanted before making the ephod, not after. The Lord has no need for gold. He owns it already. God doesn't need anything fashioned by humanity as a reminder of His character and power. The Lord made that abundantly clear generations ago in the Law given to Moses (Exod. 20:4–6). What the Lord always appreciates and never tires of receiving are our prayers, our worship, our service, our thanks and our lives. He doesn't need things to make Him happy.

THE METAL SNAKE

The Israelites must have forgotten the lesson of Moses and the bronze serpent in the wilderness of Sinai (Num. 21:9). During the Exodus the people had suffered poisonous snakebites as a punishment from God. When they looked up in faith, saw the metal snake and trusted the Lord, they were healed. Yet they took what was good to the wrong extreme, for they revered the serpent instead of the One who had healed them. They formed entire departments dedicated to maintaining the idol, not as a historic relic like the Liberty Bell at Independence Hall in Philadelphia, but as an item of sacred worship.

When the people saw the ephod, they worshipped it and not the Lord, for "all Israel prostituted themselves by worshipping it [the ephod] there, and it became a snare to Gideon and his family" (8:27). The Hebrews sold themselves by going after a cheap substitute for God's eternal love. Almost immediately they began to abandon true heart worship and sought to manipulate God to operate on their terms. Once again they preferred something tangible they could see, hold and worship rather than God, who is spirit, unseen and all-powerful.

Although Midian fell and Gideon brought peace to Israel for 40 years, he was not able to erase the damage he had done with his golden trophy. Gideon enjoyed life, had many wives and 70 sons, one of whom was Abimelech—who wanted to be king and would stop at nothing to achieve his goal. And with Abimelech things would soon go from bad to worse.

"No sooner had Gideon died than the Israelites again prostituted themselves to the Baals. They set up Baal-berith [the golden ephod] as their god and did not remember the Lord their God, who had rescued them from the hands of all their enemies on every side" (8:28–33).

We, too, do this whenever we beg God to bless the chaos we have created, and seek His guidance after we have already taken action. Clearly the Lord prefers to point us in the right direction first rather than hear our belated pleas to save us from disaster. "Lord, help me to do it right the first time because it was your idea—not mine." That response would be far superior to just trying to explain things away with a weak, "it seemed like a good idea at the time."

Worst
Promise Ever
Jephthah

ᘓᗩᘓᗩᘓ

Jephthah, still another of Israel's numerous judges, could have been a great ruler, overcoming adversity, insecurity and a poor upbringing, had he trusted completely in the Lord. He could have been a famous and revered leader, but he is remembered in Scripture for a poorly considered promise.

Following Abimelech, a series of little-known judges led Israel for 45 years. After they died, Israel slipped into its usual pattern of idolatry and disobedience. Once again the Israelites did evil in the eyes of the Lord, choosing to worship the fertility deities of the neighboring countries. Because they forsook the Lord, they were sold into the hands of the Philistines and the Ammonites, who invaded and oppressed Israel for 18 years (Judg. 10:6–8). And once again the people of Israel prayed and begged God for deliverance. What they really wanted, though, was to be rescued and then left alone so they could return to doing just as they pleased.

The Lord replied, "When the Egyptians, Amorites, Ammonites, Philistines, Sidonians, Amalekites and Maonites oppressed you and you cried to me for help, did I not save you from their hands? But you have forsaken me and served other gods, so I will no longer save you. Go and cry out to the gods you have chosen. Let them save you when you are in trouble!" (10:11–14).

CRY FOR HELP

"Okay, Lord. We know we have sinned, but now we need you to rescue us," they pleaded. As a sign of good faith they did get rid of their foreign gods—at least for a short time. And when the Lord could no longer bear the sounds of their misery, He helped them.

Desperate for decisive leadership against the Ammonites, the Israelites pledged that whoever launched an attack against their oppressors would be declared the nation's new ruler. Jephthah saw this oath as an opportunity for advancement and personal revenge. Even though he was a brave warrior and the son of Gilead, the great man whose name defined the region, his mother was a prostitute, making Jephthah an outcast in his own extended family (10:18–11:3).

It is amazing how quickly slavery changed his relatives' minds, for the very people who drove Jephthah away were the same ones who came begging for his aid. How many times has someone mistreated you and almost in the next breath asked you for a favor? How many times have we done the same thing to God?

"Didn't you hate me and drive me away from home?" Jephthah asked. "Why do you come to me now, when you're in trouble?"

"Well, times change. That was then, this is now," they replied. "Be our commander, so we can fight the Ammonites."

"If I do defeat them, will I be your leader or will you treat me the way you did before?" Jephthah further inquired.

Gilead's elders replied, "The Lord is our witness; we will certainly do as you say" (11:6–10).

Judges 11:29 says, "The Spirit of the Lord came upon Jephthah . . . and he advanced against the Ammonites" with strength to do the Lord's work. He should have immediately driven the enemy from Israel's borders without further comment. Instead, Jephthah's self-importance prompted him to blurt out a foolishly ill-advised vow.

THE VOW

"If you give the Ammonites into my hands, whatever comes out of the door of my house to meet me when I return in triumph . . . will be the Lord's, and I will sacrifice it as a burnt offering" (11:30). He made a promise that the Lord did not require or even suggest, but once made, the vow could not be rescinded.

Today we live in an era when promises are made to be broken. Sports contracts are routinely broken or merely used as starting points for new salary negotiations. God, on the other hand, expects promises to be kept. What are some of the promises you have made to the Lord and not completed? We have all made them.

When Jephthah returned home from battle, perhaps he expected to be met by some pet animal that always ran to greet him like Dino in the "Flintstones" cartoon show. When he reached home, though, the first one out the door was his daughter, his only child, singing and dancing, welcoming daddy home (11:34).

"Oh! My daughter! You have made me miserable and wretched, because I have made a vow to the Lord that I cannot break" (11:35). Note that even then he did not take responsibility for his actions. "You have made me miserable," he said—as if it were his daughter's fault.

During this time of moral, political and spiritual chaos, Jephthah's daughter seemed to be one of the few people who knew what had to be done. As far as she was concerned, a promise made is a promise kept, especially if the promise is made to God.

"Father," she replied, "you have given your word to the Lord. Do to me just as you promised" (11:36). She did request a reprieve of two months to spend with friends and to grieve for a future that would never be. At the end of the two months, the promise was fulfilled (11:37–40).

Jephthah led Israel for six years after winning the war with Ammon, but at a terrible personal cost. Imagine what he could have achieved had he not made such a foolish promise. His flawed judgment teaches us that no one sins alone or remains unaffected by the decisions of others. Sometimes we make terrible choices for which others pay the price. Sin always influences those around us, especially those closest to us. Jephthah could have been a great ruler, but he missed the opportunity.

Fortunately God made a promise before the foundation of the world, that Jesus would offer Himself as a sacrifice to pay the price and penalty of sin once and for all. That is a promise I am glad He kept.

Sorry Excuse for a King

Saul I

⊱⊰

M ost of the time personal decisions affect only a small number of people. Sometimes the general public makes a bad choice, which, added to an individual's poor choices, produces a critical mass ready to explode in chaos, confusion and conflict. Such was the case with Israel's first king—Saul.

Early in the history of Israel, God personally ruled the newly formed nation. His expectations and demands were tough, but He was fair, reliable and loving in all He did for our rebellious ancestors. Somewhere along the way, Israel began to sound like a kid who wants what all of his friends have. Because every neighboring country had a king, Israel wanted one, too. Actually, the Hebrews wanted someone who would take charge and fight their battles for them, someone who would be less demanding than the Lord. Strange that somehow in finally reaching their promised homeland, they forgot that God used to fight for them—and that He always won.

Israel prospered under a righteous leader like Samuel. But Samuel was getting old and his sons, rather than maintaining a tradition of judicial and leadership integrity, "did not walk in his ways. They turned aside after dishonest gain and accepted bribes and perverted justice" (I Sam. 8:3). So the people pleaded, begged and whined to have a king like all of their neighbors (8:5–6).

Samuel felt awful that the people had treated God with such disdain, but God assured him that he was not to blame. The Lord told
him, "Listen to all that the people are saying to you; it is not you they
have rejected, but they have rejected me as their king. As they have
done from the day I brought them up out of Egypt until this day, for-
saking me and serving other gods, so they are doing to you. Now listen to them; but warn them solemnly and let them know what the king
who will reign over them will do" (8:7–10). The people had succumbed
to the never-ending peer pressure that kids and parents still struggle
with today.

Yet unlike owning the latest designer jeans and running shoes, having
a king would be far more costly that anyone had ever imagined. Samuel,
hoping to dissuade the people from making a tragic decision that could
not be rescinded, warned them of the high price they would have to pay
living under a monarch.

> *This is what the king who will reign over you will do: He will
> take your sons and make them serve with his chariots and
> horses, and they will run in front of his chariots. Some he will
> assign to be commanders of thousands and commanders of
> fifties, and others to plow his ground and reap his harvest,
> and still others to make weapons of war and equipment for
> his chariots. He will take your daughters to be perfumers and
> cooks and bakers. He will take the best of your fields and vine-
> yards and olive groves and give them to his attendants. He
> will take a tenth of your grain and of your vintage and give it
> to his officials and attendants. Your menservants and maid-
> servants and the best of your cattle and donkeys he will take
> for his own use. He will take a tenth of your flocks, and you
> yourselves will become his slaves. When that day comes, you
> will cry out for relief from the king you have chosen, and the
> Lord will not answer you in that day* (11–18).

A MAN WITHOUT EQUAL

The Bible describes Saul, Israel's first king, as "an impressive young
man without equal among the Israelites—a head taller than any of the

others" (9:2). He was the son of Kish of the tribe of Benjamin, who was apparently a man of some reputation and status.

The Lord, in spite of being rejected and dishonored by His people, assured Samuel that all would be well. "About this time tomorrow I will send you a man from the land of Benjamin. Anoint him leader over my people Israel; he will deliver my people from the hand of the Philistines. I have looked upon my people, for their cry has reached me" (9:16).

Apart from withholding His guidance and care, sometimes the worst thing that God can do is to give us exactly what we ask for. We may find that we are more miserable than we were before. Such was the case with Saul. He began well but ended poorly because he forgot that he was supposed to be God's man, not his own.

In relaying God's promise to Saul, Samuel prophesied that, "The Spirit of the Lord will come upon you in power, and you will prophesy with them [the prophets]; and you will be changed into a different person. Once these signs are fulfilled, do whatever your hand finds to do, for God is with you" (10:6–7). As soon as Saul turned to leave, it was as if he had been marvelously transformed, because God changed not only his demeanor but his heart as well. Along with being tall and regal looking, Saul was now equipped with divine strength that no other source or advisor could provide, as long as he followed the Lord.

As Saul was entering the town of Gibeah, he met a procession of prophets. While he took note of this parade of spiritual leaders, "the Spirit of God came upon him in power, and he joined in their prophesying" (10:10). All were amazed and no doubt impressed with this young man, who seemed to be the ideal monarch. People asked, "What got into him?" Those who witnessed the transformation knew it could be nothing other than the Spirit of the Lord working in him. Too bad Saul forgot that. He thought it was all about Saul.

CORONATION

On the day of Saul's coronation, the people assembled according to tribe and waited to see who would be their new king. In order to show that the choice of king was not based on friendship or nepotism, Samuel called each tribe to see if they had a likely candidate. After checking tribe-by-tribe, clan-by-clan, family-by-family, he came to the family of Kish, Saul's father. Saul, however, was nowhere to be found. Rather than standing tall and accepting his royal commission, Saul was hunkered down behind the saddles, camel gear and suitcases hoping no one would notice him (10:21–24). The king-elect's reticence should have been the first tip-off that he was not convinced of his own appointment. And if he wasn't sure, how could the nation of Israel trust his confidence or ability?

Perhaps Samuel, a bit tongue in cheek, pointed to Saul and said, "Do you see the man the Lord has chosen? There is no one like him among all the people." But the people, seemingly oblivious to the fact that Saul had been flushed from his hiding place, responded with a hearty, "Long live the king!" (10:24). Had the Israelites realized from the outset the true quality of Saul's leadership, they probably would have all dropped to their knees to let God know that they had changed their minds about the whole king business.

Saul began well, though, because Samuel wrote down everything a king should do to serve both the nation and the citizenry. The aging prophet and judge told the people:

> If you fear the Lord and serve and obey Him and do not rebel against His commands, and if both you and the king who reigns over you follow the Lord your God—good! But if you do not obey the Lord, and if you rebel against His commands, His hand will be against you, as it was against your fathers. Now then, stand still and see this great thing the Lord is about to do before your eyes! Do not turn away after useless idols. They can do you no good, nor can they rescue you, because they are useless. For the sake of His great name the Lord will not reject His people, because the Lord was pleased to make you His own. As for me, far be it from me that I should sin against the Lord by failing to pray for you. And I will teach you the way that is good and right. But be sure to fear the Lord and serve Him faithfully with all your heart; consider what great things He has done for you. Yet if you persist in doing evil, both you and your king will be swept away (12:12–25 ff.).

Samuel's speech marked a significant if/then moment in the Bible. If you, the people obey and do what is requested with a good attitude and a willing spirit, then God will protect, bless, encourage and sustain you. But if not, all bets are off.

Samuel dismissed the people and went home—retired to private life as we would call it now. Saul, it is recorded, was 30 years old when he became king and reigned for 42 years (13:1). When Samuel left he may have offered a short prayer for the Lord's intervention—"May the Lord help them all—they are going to need it."

WAR

Early in Saul's reign, Israel went to war with Philistia. As Israel's commander-in-chief, Saul mustered an army of 3,000 men. He had 2,000 soldiers with him at Michmash and another 1,000 with his son Jonathan at Gibeah. Any stragglers or those on sick call he dismissed to return home (13:2). His dismissal explains the primary reason why Israel wanted a king—to raise an army, lead it into battle and deliver the nation from all her enemies—so the people could stay home and safely run their farms, families and businesses.

Saul and Jonathan went on the offensive after the Philistines, but they were clearly outnumbered. "The Philistines assembled to fight Israel with 3,000 chariots, 6,000 charioteers, and soldiers as numerous as the sand on the seashore" (13:5). Inverting a well-known principle of leadership, "When the going gets tough; the tough get going," the mantra for Saul's army became "When the going gets tough, the tough run for their lives!"

"When the men of Israel saw that their situation was critical and that their army was hard pressed, they hid in caves and thickets, among the rocks, and in pits and cisterns. Some Hebrews even crossed the Jordan to the land of Gad and Gilead. Saul remained at Gilgal, and all the troops with him were quaking with fear" (13:6–7). They had lost confidence in their country, their army and their king and were running scared, hiding wherever they could disappear, even in snake and scorpion filled holes in the ground.

SACRIFICE

Saul needed Samuel to offer a sacrifice and to seek the Lord's guidance before the situation worsened. But Samuel didn't come. Saul waited seven days, as the two men had agreed, but Samuel still did not arrive. As more and more soldiers deserted with each passing day, Israel's army reached the brink of collapse. The wheels were falling off the royal coach of state and everyone, including Saul, knew it.

The king said, "Bring me the burnt offering and the fellowship offerings," (13:9) and he offered the sacrifices himself in place of the Lord's appointed priests. And just as surely as the phone rings once you get into the bathtub, Samuel arrived—and he was not happy.

Saul went out to greet the prophet, no doubt feeling pleased with his initiative and his assertive response to the military crisis. Rather than congratulate Saul, though, Samuel was furious.

"What have you done?" he demanded (13:11). Saul blurted out an abbreviated rationale by shifting the blame away from his deed onto Samuel's lateness. "When I saw that the men were scattering, and that you did not come at the set time, and that the Philistines were assembling at Michmash, I thought, *Now the Philistines will come down against me at Gilgal, and I have not sought the Lord's favor.* So I felt *compelled* (author's emphasis) to offer the burnt offering" (13:11–12).

Essentially Saul blamed Samuel for the problem. Saul needed to consult the Lord and seek His favor, and because Samuel was not there to do it, Saul went ahead and did it himself. "You acted foolishly," Samuel replied. "You have not kept the command the Lord your God gave you; if you had, He would have established your kingdom over Israel for all time. But now your kingdom will not endure; the Lord has sought out a man after His own heart and appointed him leader of His people, because you have not kept the Lord's command" (13:13).

Not only was Saul wrong for presuming to know the mind of God, he did not show any evidence of basic trust in the Lord. And just as God had chosen Saul to give the people what they asked for, He just as surely planned to remove him, not by recall, impeachment or forced abdication, but by allowing his disobedience to run its course, ruining everything it touched.

The Lord did honor Saul's son, Jonathan, and his men, who won a victory over the Philistines (13:15–14:23). Had Saul seen the victory coming purely by the Lord's intervention, he might have saved his kingship by seeking forgiveness for the sacrifice and trying to be the best king he could possibly be. True to form, he accepted the glory for himself and made yet another bad decision.

Point of No Return
Saul II

~∽◎◎∽

Before Israel's army could bury their dead and tend to their wounded following the battle with the Philistines, Saul issued a royal decree that carried the force of law, "Cursed be any man who eats food before evening comes, before I have avenged myself on my enemies!" (I Samuel 14:24). His edict failed to glorify God for the victory, and it offered no compassion for the soldiers who were famished.

When the king's army passed through a section of woods, they found an abundance of wild honey (14:25–26). So with food close at hand and free for the taking, the entire army passed it by and went hungry.

Jonathan, however, had not heard the order. When he passed the area, he stopped to take advantage of the free source of carbohydrates. Refreshed, invigorated and ready to resume the fight, he was surprised to hear one of his soldiers say, "Your father bound the army under a strict oath, saying, 'Cursed be any man who eats food today!' That is why the men are faint" (14:28).

Realizing his father's mistake, Jonathan said, "My father has made trouble for the country. See how my eyes brightened when I tasted a little of this honey. How much better it would have been if the men had eaten today some of the plunder they took from their enemies. Would not the slaughter of the Philistines have been even greater?" (14:29–30).

Later that day the Israelites returned to fight the Philistines and beat them soundly all the way from Micmash to Aijalon. But they were physically, spiritually and emotionally exhausted. When the Philistines withdrew, the famished Israelites "pounced on the plunder and, taking sheep, cattle and calves, they butchered them on the ground and ate them, together with the blood" (14:32). The Hebrews believed that life was in the blood, and under the Law it was a sin to eat any meat with blood in it.

Amid the confusion of the mass barbecue, someone came to Saul and said, "Look, the men are sinning against the Lord by eating meat that has blood in it" (14:33). In response he called for a large boulder to be rolled over and for the people to slaughter their animals correctly.

Saul then built an altar to the Lord for the first time. His game plan was to go after the Philistines and annihilate them: "Let us go down after the Philistines by night and plunder them till dawn, and let us not leave one of them alive" (14:36).

The priests agreed that it was better to seek the Lord's guidance before Saul ordered a new battle plan that might be catastrophic. So Saul asked God whether he should attack and wipe out the Philistines. Scripture says that God did not answer (14:37). In almost every other reference to prayer, God always answers. Not this time. Saul prayed, asked and perhaps even pleaded for the Lord's advice, and received only silence. Rather than admit his error, he stumbled blindly ahead on his own.

Finally, Samuel returned to the wayward king to deliver a message from the Lord. The Lord may have been silent to Saul, but fortunately for the country, God still spoke through Samuel. "This is what the Lord Almighty says: 'I will punish the Amalekites for what they did to Israel when they waylaid them as they came up from Egypt. Now go, attack the Amalekites and totally destroy everything that belongs to them. Do not spare them; put to death men and women, children and infants, cattle and sheep, camels and donkeys'" (15:2–3).

SPOILS OF WAR

King Saul assembled an army—200,000 foot soldiers and 10,000 men from Judah—and set off to Amalek to deliver an ambush and carry out the Lord's command (15:4). He attacked the Amalekites "all the way from Havilah to Shur, to the east of Egypt" (15:7). Once again Saul responded with an incomplete obedience that bordered on dereliction of duty. Saul "took Agag king of the Amalekites alive, and all his people he totally destroyed with the sword. But Saul and the army spared Agag and the best of the sheep and cattle, the fat calves and lambs—everything that was good. These they were unwilling to destroy completely, but everything that was despised and weak they totally destroyed" (15:8).

God was not pleased. The Lord told Samuel: "I am grieved that I have made Saul king, because he has turned away from me and has not carried out my instructions" (15:10).

There is a scene in the Academy award winning film, "The Lord of the Rings," where the king of Rohan, sending his people to fight against huge armies of evil massed to ensure their annihilation, asks, "How did it come to this?" The answer is that it came to this from years of neglect and allowing disobedience to go unchecked.

LOWERING THE BOOM

Deeply troubled on hearing the news of God's displeasure, Samuel prayed all night, asking the Lord for guidance. After a long night of anguish, he went to meet Saul to "lower the boom" on God's behalf. Saul had gone to Carmel to erect a monument to himself, and then he traveled down to Gilgal (15:12). As soon as he saw Samuel coming he exclaimed with great self-satisfaction, "The Lord bless you! I have carried out the Lord's instructions" (15:13).

As Saul stood there dreaming about his statue, Samuel demanded, "What then is this bleating of sheep in my ears? What is this lowing of cattle that I hear?" (15:15). Sounding eerily reminiscent of Aaron when confronted about the golden calf, Saul explained, "The soldiers brought them from the Amalekites; they spared the best of the sheep and cattle to sacrifice to the Lord your God, but we totally destroyed the rest" (15:15). He tried to shift the blame and responsibility for his actions onto the soldiers, but it was his fault. It was at his command, on his watch, and as such, he was ultimately responsible for the actions of the army and those under his authority.

SAMUEL'S LAMENT

Samuel, in no mood to hear Saul's' litany of lame excuses, cut short the conversation. Instead, he relayed the Lord's message and reminded

Saul of how the Lord had chosen him to be king. "Although you were once small in your own eyes, did you not become the head of the tribes of Israel? The Lord anointed you king over Israel. And He sent you on a mission, saying, 'Go and completely destroy those wicked people, the Amalekites; make war on them until you have wiped them out.' Why did you not obey the Lord? Why did you pounce on the plunder and do evil in the eyes of the Lord?" (15:16–19).

"But I did obey the Lord," Saul stated as forcefully as he could, sensing his reign slipping away. "I went on the mission the Lord assigned me and completely destroyed the Amalekites and brought back Agag their king." He went on to say that it was the soldiers who took the livestock to present a sacrifice to the Lord.

Samuel replied: "Does the Lord delight in burnt offerings and sacrifices as much as in obeying the voice of the Lord? To obey is better than sacrifice, and to heed is better than the fat of rams. For rebellion is like the sin of divination, and arrogance like the evil of idolatry. Because you have rejected the word of the Lord, He has rejected you as king" (15:22–23).

Although sacrifice mattered in establishing a right relationship between Israel and God, what God wanted above all was obedience. The Lord greatly desires a willing obedience that springs from love, and reverence expressing our worship and gratitude for His goodness.

Saul appears to have repented and immediately sought the Lord's forgiveness. In reality, he was not sorry for making God look bad, but for being found out and looking bad himself. Saul said to Samuel, "I have sinned. I violated the Lord's command and your instructions. I was afraid of the people and so I gave in to them. Now I beg you, forgive my sin and come back with me, so that I may worship the Lord" (15:24–25). He wanted Samuel to return with him to show the people that he was still the king and worthy to be Israel's leader. But by then, he had officially worn out his welcome as far as the Lord was concerned.

PANIC

Samuel told Saul that he would not accompany him and that because he had rejected the Lord's instructions, God had rejected him as king over Israel (15:26). Then Saul panicked. He had lost face, lost the kingdom and lost the respect of his army. He was desperate to salvage what remained of his dignity and position. So as Samuel turned to leave, Saul, pleading for his kingship, grabbed the hem of Samuel's robe and accidentally tore it. With that ripping away of fabric, Saul could almost hear the ripping away of his kingdom, and his life came crashing down around him.

Samuel said, "The Lord has torn the kingdom of Israel from you today and has given it to one of your neighbors—to one better than you. He who is the Glory of Israel does not lie or change his mind; for He is not a man, that He should change His mind" (15:28–29). Saul had the appearance but not the substance of leadership.

One last time Saul appeared to confess his sin. He intended to have Samuel accompany him to worship so the masses would have no idea that the king was on the slippery slope out of royalty. He wanted the honor without the requisite humility of character. "I have sinned. But please honor me before the elders of my people."

Samuel, to his credit, did not shame the king in front of the troops and briefly went with him to worship. He then called for the prisoner Agag of Amalek to be brought to him. Samuel executed the king of Amalek, completing what Saul should have already done.

That was the last time Saul reaped the benefit of Samuel's advice and his relationship with God, for "until the day Samuel died, he did not go to see Saul again, though Samuel mourned for him. And the Lord was grieved that He had made Saul king over Israel" (15:35). King Saul was almost a complete washout as a king. He failed to offer a right sacrifice, and he disobeyed the Lord as to the fate of Agag and the Amalekites. By not completely eliminating the Amalekites, Saul helped to create and sustain an animosity that continued for millennia.

Once again the Philistines gathered for war. By now though, Samuel was dead and the whole nation mourned him. They needed someone who could lead them safely to victory. Instead, all they had was Saul—tall, inept, arrogant Saul.

THE MEDIUM OF ENDOR

King Saul felt desperate without either Samuel or the Lord to advise him in his time of crisis. By that time he "had expelled the mediums and spiritists from the land" (28:3) so there was not even a pagan seer left to offer advice. When Saul saw the Philistine army, he was nearly paralyzed with fear and indecision. He prayed, but the Lord did not answer. He pleaded, but the Lord did not respond through a prophet or with dreams or visions. The frantic king called together some of his advisors and demanded, "Find me a woman who is a medium, so I may go and inquire of her" (28:7). They found one in Endor and the king arranged a meeting with her.

Saul changed into a disguise and went at night to find the woman. "Consult a spirit for me," he said, "and bring up for me the one I name" (28:8). Thinking that this might be a trap and that she might be arrested, initially the medium refused. But once the king assured her that she was in no danger, she agreed and asked who she was to contact "on the other side."

When Saul asked to speak to Samuel, she screamed, "Why have you deceived me? You are Saul!" (28:11) For he was the only person in the entire kingdom with the temerity to awaken one of Israel's greatest spiritual leaders through a medium.

The medium saw a spirit, dressed like an old man in a robe, coming up out of the ground. Saul immediately knew it was Samuel and rushed to bow low before him. Saul said, "I am in great distress. The Philistines are fighting against me, and God has turned away from me. He no longer answers me, either by prophets or by dreams. So I have called on you to tell me what to do" (28:15).

Samuel, mightily irked at having his eternal rest disturbed, especially by Saul, said, "Why have you disturbed me by bringing me up? Why do you consult me, now that the Lord has turned away from you and become your enemy? The Lord has done what He predicted through me. The Lord has torn the kingdom out of your hands and given it to one of your neighbors—to David.

"Because you did not obey the Lord or carry out His fierce wrath against the Amalekites, the Lord has done this to you today. The Lord will hand over both Israel and you to the Philistines, and tomorrow you and your sons will be with me. The Lord will also hand over the army of Israel to the Philistines" (28:16–19).

PHILISTINE VICTORY

Saul never got it. The Lord made him king and honored him with a place and reputation far above any one else in the kingdom. Even so, he always chose to do exactly what he wanted despite all the instructions and warnings he received. The next day he went into battle with his sons, Jonathan, Abinadab and Malki-shua, at Mount Gilboa. All three sons were killed in action, and Saul was critically wounded in the battle.

Rather than be taken prisoner and at least die like a king, Saul asked his armor bearer to strike him down. But the armor bearer, fearing even a wounded king, refused. In desperation, Israel's first king fell on his sword and took his own life. When his armor bearer saw that Saul was dead, he fell on his sword and died with him (31:1–5).

The next day, when the Philistines came to strip the dead, they found the bodies of Saul and his three sons. "They cut off his head and stripped off his armor, and they sent messengers throughout the land of the Philistines to proclaim the news in the temple of their idols and among their people" (31:8–9).

No one sins alone, for each decision contrary to God's plan influences those around us, often with disastrous consequences. Saul, his sons and many of Israel's finest young men died that day exactly as Samuel had predicted—not because of the Philistines—but because of Saul's history of poor decisions that cost him his family, his honor, his throne and his life.

Plausible Deniability

David I

⌘

Because of an endless litany of scandals in the government of the United States, the television viewing public has added a new phrase to the lexicon of American politics—plausible deniability.

Plausible deniability refers to the denial of blame in a covert government operation. The operation is usually so arcane and complex that should anyone be implicated, no direct connection can be made to the president or any other high-ranking government official. If the perpetrators are caught, there must be a reasonable and believable excuse so that no involvement can be traced back to top decision makers.

This is not a new idea. Coming up with a good excuse is as old as Adam and Eve—"the woman . . . she gave me some fruit . . . and I ate it" (Gen. 3:12). Although there are numerous cases of plausible deniability in Scripture, perhaps one of the most notable is the scandalous affair between King David and Bathsheba as recorded in II Samuel 11–12. This sordid scheme led its participants down the path of temptation, deception, adultery, conspiracy and murder—all within the context of plausible deniability.

A SECOND LOOK

King David, unable to sleep, had taken a walk in the cool of the night up on his roof-top terrace. Perhaps he had too much caffeine before going to bed or he felt anxious about the prospect of war or an internal attack on his administration. From the rooftop he spotted the lovely Bathsheba taking a bath on top of the adjacent building. David ogled, leered and lusted and then he instructed his chief of staff, Joab, to begin a covert operation to bring Bathsheba over to the palace for a royal rendezvous.

Joab, though, needed to handle the matter with secrecy and discretion, for how would it look for the king of Israel, a man hand-picked by God, to be linked to an affair with a married woman? They all knew the punishment if they were discovered—death by stoning.

When Bathsheba became pregnant, David and Joab crafted a covert plan to ensure that the child David had fathered could not be linked to him. But Uriah, Bathsheba's husband and a loyal soldier, stymied the king's loathsome scheme by refusing to return home while his men were still camped out on the field of battle. Had he gone home to Bathsheba, the child would have been presumed to be Uriah's, not David's.

Once Uriah had upended the royal plan, more drastic measures became necessary. In the jargon of spying and secrets, Uriah was "expendable" in order to maintain the king's image and ensure plausible deniability. But rather than assassinate Uriah, or "terminate him with extreme prejudice," David decided to place him in the thick of battle so that he had no chance of survival. Poor Uriah was posted on the front lines, cut off from support and killed just as surely as if Joab or David had murdered him with their own hands.

After suitably pious eulogies and posthumous decorations for bravery "above and beyond the call of duty," all of the guilty parties hoped that the Uriah problem would soon be forgotten. David observed a respectable period of mourning and then took the poor, apparently grief-stricken Bathsheba to be his wife. The public praised the king's compassion and rejoiced that the child on the way was an apparent blessing from the Lord. But they didn't know the truth of the king's dirty secret.

REPENTANCE

With Uriah dead, David and Bathsheba pledged to mutual silence, and no witnesses to tell the real story, it seemed that David was in the clear, that is, until the prophet Nathan confronted him. To David's credit, he did not continue his policy of plausible deniability. Rather than cover up, deny or excuse his actions, he confessed his sin to God and immediately asked for forgiveness. In his anguish he probably penned one of his most famous psalms:

"Have mercy on me, O God, according to your unfailing love; according to your great compassion blot out my transgressions. Wash away all my iniquity and cleanse me from my sin. For I know my transgressions, and my sin is always before me. Against you, you only, have I sinned and done what is evil in your sight . . . Create in me a pure heart, O God, and renew a steadfast spirit within me. Do not cast me from your presence or take your Holy Spirit from me. Restore to me the joy of your salvation and grant me a willing spirit, to sustain me" (Ps. 51:1–4; 10–12).

David was forgiven, but he didn't get away with his sin. His policy of plausible deniability did not work. And it will not work for us either, since deniability, regardless of how plausible or justifiable it may seem to be, is still rebellion and disobedience against God.

We may be quick to blame others so poor performance cannot be traced back to us. After all, we cannot be held responsible if someone else was at fault. Our situations may not lead to murder, but they may still create problems in our relationship with God and each other.

We may think that we have hidden our faults and bad attitudes so well that even God will not be able to trace them back to us. But Scripture tells us that this idea is as wrong for us as it was for King David. "You have sinned against the Lord; and be sure your sin will find you out" (Num. 32:23).

It is far better to live in loving obedience to God, who saves us from sin. Plausible deniability, or any other kind of deniability, just doesn't work.

Counting Heads
David II

ejoge

As bad as the adultery, conspiracy and murder of Uriah had been, King David was about to make a choice that would have still direr consequences. The affair with Bathsheba ended with the king being humiliated and exposed by the prophet Nathan. The baby born to David and Bathsheba died. But in this case David's decisions and actions affected a fairly small number of people. He would soon make a choice that would have much wider repercussions.

David opted for a census of Israel and Judah, not to determine the need for new schools, roads and sports facilities, or even to help access and maximize the tax base. The purpose of the census was to ascertain the number of men who were available to defend the country in the event of war. But Israel belonged to God, not to David, and only God could order an accounting of troops (II Sam. 24:1–2).

COUNTING THE TROOPS

The biblical account of the origin of the census differs according to the source we cite. I Chronicles 21:1 tells us that, "Satan rose up against Israel and incited David to take a census." But in II Samuel 24:1, we read that it was God's anger burning against Israel that drove David to count heads. In any case, David told his chief of staff, Joab, and all of the army commanders, "Go throughout the tribes of Israel from Dan to Beersheba and enroll the fighting men, so that I may know how many there are" (II Sam. 24:2). The phrase "Dan to Beersheba," was the Israelite counterpart of "from Maine to California" in the United States.

Joab, at least, expressed a reluctance to count the fighting men. He indicated his surety that at any given point, in response to the need, God would multiply David's fighting force "a hundred times over . . . why does my lord the king want to do such a thing?" (II Sam. 23:3). Joab may have suspected that the military census was motivated largely by the pride and vanity of King David. Late in his reign, David may have wanted to bask in the glory of the amazing growth and prosperity of Israel. Joab did not include the tribes of Levi and Benjamin in the numbering, "because the king's command was repulsive to him." (I Chronicles 21:6).

David's lack of trust was also evil in the sight of God. God never wanted Saul or David or any other king to make decisions apart from Him. He did not want Israel to rely on strength of arms to accomplish political policy. David even voiced that theme in one of his many psalms:

> *May the Lord answer you when you are in distress; may the name of the God of Jacob protect you. May He send you help from the sanctuary and grant you support from Zion. May He remember all your sacrifices and accept your burnt offerings. May He give you the desire of your heart and make all your plans succeed. We will shout for joy when you are victorious and will lift up our banners in the name of our God. May the Lord grant all your requests. Now I know that the Lord saves His anointed; He answers him from His holy heaven with the saving power of His right hand. Some trust in chariots and some in horses, but we trust in the name of the Lord our God* (Ps. 20:2–7).

David wrote it, but he didn't adhere to it, for he overruled Joab and his staff and ordered the census to proceed. After traveling the length and breadth of Israel and taking nine months and 20 days to complete the tally, palace officials returned to Jerusalem with the final count—"In Israel there were 800,000 able-bodied men who could handle a sword, and in Judah 500,000" (II Sam. 24:8–9). A total of 1.3 million men would make Israel the first super-power in the Middle East, formidable enough to face any enemy who tried to encroach upon her borders.

Shortly after all the data had been collected, collated and prepared for his generals, David had second thoughts about what he had done. In fact, he was wracked by guilt and robbed of sleep and peace. David prayed, "Lord, I have sinned greatly in what I have done. Now, O Lord, I beg you, take away the guilt of your servant. I have done a very foolish thing" (24:10).

In humility David admitted his disobedience before a prophet could come forward and confront him with it. He knew he was wrong from the start. It didn't take long, though, for the Lord to respond to David's prayer. The next morning, right after David awoke, showered, and ate breakfast, the king's seer, Gad the prophet, came into the throne room to deliver some bad news. His grim prediction sounds eerily like the old "Let's Make A Deal" game show—you can choose what is behind door number one, door number two or door number three. In this case, however, there was no gag gift, new car or wonderful vacation package to be found.

DOOR NUMBER THREE

The prophet unveiled the choices and gave David an opportunity to make his selection. No matter which one he picked, though, innocent people would pay the price for his arrogance and stupidity. Gad told David, "Shall there come upon you three years of famine in your land? Or three months of fleeing from your enemies while they pursue you? Or three days of plague in your land? Now then, think it over and decide how I should answer the One who sent me" (24:13).

We make choices every day—what to wear, what to eat, where to go, what to do. Rarely though, do any of those affect an entire population. David had to consider his options—three years of famine, three months living on the run from his enemies or a plague of three days that might kill thousands of people. If he ran, Israel could face a *coup d'etat* that might plunge the country into a civil war.

His third option was slightly better. For three days there would be a plague. We have seen the results of bubonic plague in the Middle Ages, which killed one third of the entire population of Europe. Likewise, the Ebola virus and the HIV/AIDS virus have unleashed incredible terror, misery and death.

David admitted, "I am in deep distress." But he also knew that it was far better to "fall into the hands of the Lord, for his mercy is great; but do not let me fall into the hands of men" (24:14). David did not want to subject the country to civil war or condemn the population to years of lingering death. Almost by default, he opted for the plague since it was of relatively short duration. Days could be endured; years would have been unbearable.

PLAGUE

"So the Lord sent a plague on Israel from that morning until the end of the time designated, and 70,000 of the people from Dan to Beersheba died" (24:15).

As the angel of death was preparing to destroy Jerusalem, "the Lord was grieved because of the calamity and said to the angel who was afflicting the people, 'Enough! Withdraw your hand'" (24:16). David saw the angel there at the threshing floor of Araunah the Jebusite, a well-known landmark. He said to the Lord, "I am the one who has sinned and done wrong. These are but sheep. What have they done? Let your hand fall upon me and my family" (24:17). David did not just sweat out three days of pestilence from the relative safety of his private palace; he took responsibility for his part in this national crisis. He was willing to let himself and his family suffer if the rest of Israel could be spared. Even after the foolish choice he made, he showed that he still had the heart and soul to be the Lord's king.

God ordered David to go to the threshing floor, buy the place and there offer sacrifices to the Lord. That same location in Jerusalem later became the site of the great Temple. This time David did as he was commanded. He "built an altar to the Lord there and sacrificed burnt offerings and fellowship offerings. Then the Lord answered prayer in behalf of the land, and the plague on Israel was stopped" (24:25).

Too bad David didn't make that choice before he cost 70,000 innocent people their lives.

Just Trying to Be Helpful

Uzzah

The next bad decision is difficult to understand because it seems so out of character for God. It makes the Lord seem arbitrary, unkind and unfair. And if there is anything that particularly irks the American mindset about how life should be lived, unfairness rankles our sensibilities the most. Perhaps the old adage, "No good deed goes unpunished" had its beginnings with Uzzah.

In I Chronicles 13, we learn that following the plague, David bought the property in Jerusalem that would be the location for the Tabernacle and eventually the Temple. He then ordered the ark of the covenant to be taken out of storage and brought to Jerusalem. It was the same ark that had housed the pot of manna, Aaron's rod and the engraved tablets of stone with the Law—all to be kept in the Holy of Holies in the Tabernacle. Over the years, through a series of wars and neglect, the ark had been stashed away in the house of Abinadab for safe keeping (I Chron. 13:7). David recognized the sacredness of the ark, and he wanted to bring it to Jerusalem, the center of worship for Israel.

This time, seeking to avoid repeating his earlier sin of arrogant presumption, David consulted his advisors as to the appropriate course of action. He announced to the people: "If it seems good to you and if it is the will of the Lord our God, let us send word far and wide to the rest of our brothers throughout the territories of Israel, and also to the priests and Levites who are with them in their towns and pasturelands, to come and join us. Let us bring the ark of our God back to us, for we did not inquire of it during the reign of Saul" (13:2–3).

MACY'S PARADE

The king, with a large contingent of dignitaries and priests, joyfully retrieved the ark from Kiriath Jearim and began the long procession to Jerusalem. They moved the ark from Abinadab's house on a special cart, with Uzzah and Ahio leading the convoy.

What a procession that must have been! Imagine the Tournament of Roses Parade, Macy's Thanksgiving Day Parade and the rest of the biggest and brightest parades all rolled into one. "David and all the Israelites were celebrating with all their might before God, with songs and with harps, lyres, tambourines, cymbals and trumpets" (13:8). Maybe there were marching bands, twirlers, acrobats, horses and floats too, with David as the grand marshal riding in his version of a flower-draped antique touring car.

SPLIT-SECOND DECISION

Just as the cart carrying the ark reached the threshing floor area, the oxen stumbled and Uzzah tried to steady the ark to keep it from falling off the cart and hitting the ground. What follows next is shocking, to say the least. Scripture says that "the Lord's anger burned against Uzzah, and He struck him down because he had put his hand on the ark. So he died there before God" (13:10). Uzzah was zapped dead right then and there. Poor Uzzah made a split-second decision that cost him his life as surely as if he had grabbed a live high-voltage electrical cable.

King David, angry that God had killed Uzzah without warning, was afraid to move the ark or even come near it. He decided not to bring the ark into Jerusalem but to take it to the house of Obed-edom the Gittite, where it remained for three months. During that time, however, the Lord blessed Obed-edom and his entire family (13:12–14). One man gets toasted while another is blessed—how confusing is that? We turn to the history behind the ark to help us understand why Uzzah may have met this seemingly unjust fate.

The purpose of the Ark was to help the people appreciate the presence and availability of God. At the top of the ark, where the wings of the cherubim touched, stood the mercy seat. In Exodus 25:22 we read that the presence of God dwelt above the mercy seat between two cherubim, and there God and His people could meet. There once a year the High Priest entered the Holy of Holies on the Day of Atonement to place the blood of an offering that covered the sins of the people. The ark was where God came to meet His people to confront their sins, which gave it a tremendous source of power.

During the Exodus from Egypt, the ark was to be carried and cared for by the Levites—the priestly class. The priests "were responsible for the care of the ark, the table, the lamp stand, the altars, the articles of the sanctuary used in ministering, the curtain, and everything related to their use" (Num. 3:31).

They had strict orders on how to carry and cover the ark. The Lord told Moses: "Tell your brother Aaron [the first high priest] not to come whenever he chooses into the Most Holy Place behind the curtain in front of the atonement cover on the ark, or else he will die, because I appear in the cloud over the atonement cover" (Lev. 16:2). Therefore, if even the high priest could not go near the ark, it was doubly dangerous for Uzzah to do so.

When the Israelites crossed over the Jordan River into Canaan, the priests carried the ark ahead of the people. As soon as their feet touched the water, the river stopped flowing so they could all cross on dry land (Josh. 3:1–4:24). The priests and the army marched around the city in silence for six days. On the seventh day, the army blew trumpets, the walls fell flat, and then the Israelites destroyed the city of Jericho (Josh. 6:1–21).

After Moses and Joshua died, Israel desperately needed a strong leader who could keep the country united. In order to maintain stability, protect the innocent and save Israel from its enemies, God appointed judges for relatively short intervals of time. During one of many wars that Israel fought with the Philistines, the Israelite army brought the ark from its resting place in Shiloh out to the battlefield, where the Hebrews began to worship it like a divine good luck charm. They perceived the ark as a power generator that would kill all of their enemies, especially the Philistines.

CAPTURING THE ARK

But the Philistines captured the ark and in the process killed 30,000 Israelite soldiers (I Sam. 4:1–11). They took the ark to Ashdod and Ekron in Philistia, and one day they placed it in the temple beside their pagan god, Dagon. When they arose early the next morning, they found Dagon laying face down before the ark of the Lord. Perhaps thinking there had been a strong wind or earthquake during the night, they put Dagon's image back in its place. Sure enough, the next day the statue was face down again, except this time only the body remained intact—the arms and legs were broken off—as if Dagon had bowed in submission to the Almighty. They didn't try to stand it up a third time (I Sam. 5:2–5).

The Lord wasn't through with the Philistines just yet, for Scripture says, "The Lord's hand was heavy upon the people of Ashdod and its vicinity; He brought devastation upon them and afflicted them with tumors" (5:6). Some scholars believe this disease might have caused the discoloration and swelling of lymph nodes that later besieged Europe during outbreaks of the Bubonic plague.

Noting that one day they were all healthy and the next they were dying horrible deaths, the Philistines drew a direct correlation between the arrival of the ark and the onset of pestilence. They said, "The ark of the God of Israel must not stay here with us, because His hand is heavy upon us and upon Dagon our god" (5:7).

The Philistines moved the ark to Gath, but that was not far enough because Gath was still in Philistine territory. And, as soon as it was moved, the Lord redoubled the plague, afflicting young and old and throwing the city into a panic. In desperation they tried taking the ark to Ekron but when they arrived there the people shouted, "They have brought the ark of the God of Israel around to us to kill us and our people. Send the ark of the God of Israel away; let it go back to its own place, or it will kill us and our people" (5:8–6:1). With the ark in Philistine territory for seven months, there must have been great suffering and loss of life.

Philistine experts and priests then decided to put the ark on a new cart with a brand new set of oxen and a substantial offering of gold, hoping that God would lift the disease that was ravaging the country. They knew about the ten plagues that had once afflicted the Egyptians, and were in no mood to see the wrath of God repeated in their country.

BACK TO ISRAEL

The Philistines loaded up the cart with the ark and the offerings and turned it loose out in the boondocks, breathing a sigh of relief when the oxen made the slow turn heading back into Israelite territory. The oxen and their odd cargo came to a halt in the field of a man named Joshua in Beth Shemesh. There the Levites took possession of the ark and offered sacrifices to God in thanks for its safe return. The Levites had to take care of the ark, for to have someone else handle it would have meant certain death—as it did for the Philistines, Uzzah and 70 men of Beth Shemesh who dared to look inside it and were killed.

Shortly after the return of the ark, the people of Beth Shemesh transferred it to Abinidab's house on the hill, and "consecrated Eleazar his son to guard the ark of the Lord. It was a long time, 20 years in all, that the ark remained at Kiriath Jearim, and all the people of Israel mourned and sought after the Lord" (6:8–7:2).

Was Uzzah showing off? Was he not living in right relationship and obedience to the Lord? Probably he was not a Levite priest and therefore unauthorized to touch the ark. In any case, God established his holiness and majesty while showing that He can take care of Himself. When we do something good for the Lord and think we are doing Him a favor, we should remember the ark. Some things should never be touched—fruit from the tree of the knowledge of good and evil, sin in any form and the ark of the covenant (Indiana Jones and "Raiders of the Lost Ark" notwithstanding).

A Wild Looking Bird

Nebuchadnezzar

⤸⟲⟳⤹

A nyone used to the finer things in life has probably enjoyed the privilege of a good education—learning the classics, literature, math, philosophy, political science, history and the natural sciences—with the intent of becoming generally well informed. One might hope that people of nobility would be highly intelligent and able to make good decisions. Unfortunately, though, royal birth and the wisdom to make good choices are not always mutually compatible. This was certainly true of King Nebuchadnezzar of Babylon, who seems to have had a grandiose sense of his own importance and ability.

One night the king dreamed that he became crazy and was set loose to live in the wild. Believing the dream was a message sent from God, He called in Daniel to interpret the prophecy.

SEVEN SEASONS

Daniel told the king that because of his inflated ego, the Lord would punish him for a period of "seven seasons." In the Bible the number seven is always associated with God and completion. This number probably meant seven growing seasons of planting, growing, harvesting, recovery, or roughly a year in duration. It allowed just enough time for God to get Nebuchadnezzar's undivided attention in preparation for a major adjustment in his attitude. Apparently the Lord saw something redeemable in him and had decided to teach him a valuable lesson.

As King Nebuchadnezzar was walking around the flat roof of the royal palace in Babylon one day, he began thinking, "Is not this the great Babylon I have built as the royal residence, by my mighty power and for the glory of my majesty?" (Dan. 4:29–30). He looked around at everything he had ordered built as a monument to the glory of Babylon—the hanging gardens, palaces, temples, government offices, memorials, tourist attractions, shopping malls, condominium complexes, multiplex cinemas, interstate highways, and "7-11" type convenience stores—more for the glory of Nebuchadnezzar than the Babylonian empire.

Before his tribute to his own greatness could fade away, a voice came from the sky above saying, "This is what is decreed for you, King Nebuchadnezzar: Your royal authority has been taken from you. You will be driven away from people and will live with the wild animals; you will eat grass like cattle. Seven times will pass by for you until you acknowledge that the Most High is sovereign over the kingdoms of men and gives them to anyone He wishes" (4:31–32).

Scripture says that the prophecy was completed immediately—no waiting, no interpretation, no Senate hearings, no CNN headlines. The king went nuts right before everyone's eyes. Where he had been elegantly dressed and well-spoken, he immediately became a disheveled and dangerous looking mess. His constituents, fearing that the madness might be contagious, gave him the bum's rush out of town.

In his dementia, the king ate grass like cattle. He was dirty, foul smelling and soaked from the morning dew. He let his appearance go until his hair and shaggy beard looked like feathers and his finger and toenails looked like a bird's claws (4:33). What a wild looking bird he must have made!

REPENTANCE

King Nebuchadnezzar remained mad for seven measurable periods of time until he finally decided to reorder his priorities. He repented. He did a 180° turn in his thinking, attitude and obedience. He knew he had sinned and was not just sorry for being caught and punished. He was sorry enough to change and to go in the right direction.

God took away all that Nebuchadnezzar held dear—palace, wealth, security, intelligence, status, popularity, position. Nebuchadnezzar, who thought he deserved the treatment of royalty, ended up with nothing but his insane thoughts and his guilt until he came to accept the sovereignty of God. When he did he was restored to prominence with greater authority and influence than ever.

The book of Daniel says: "At the end of that time, I, Nebuchadnezzar, raised my eyes toward heaven, and my sanity was restored. Then I praised the Most High; I honored and glorified Him who lives forever. His dominion is an eternal dominion; His kingdom endures from generation to generation. All the peoples of the earth are regarded as nothing. He does as He pleases with the powers of heaven and the peoples of the earth. No one can hold back His hand or say to Him: 'What have you done?'

"At the same time that my sanity was restored, my honor and splendor were returned to me for the glory of my kingdom. My advisers and nobles sought me out, and I was restored to my throne and became even greater than before. Now I, Nebuchadnezzar, praise and exalt and glorify the King of heaven, because everything He does is right and all His ways are just. And those who walk in pride He is able to humble" (Dan. 4:34–37).

Nebuchadnezzar had to learn that the Lord could just as quickly humble him as exalt him. A valuable lesson for us all who tend to place our trust in our looks, affluence, intellect and charm. Anybody need a haircut and a manicure, Nebuchadnezzar style?

It's Not About You

King Belshazzar

⤜❦⤛

James, the brother of Jesus and a pillar in the early Church, commands us: "Humble yourselves before the Lord, and He will lift you up" (James 4:10). It is too bad that Belshazzar, Nebuchadnezzar's son and heir, did not learn from his father's experience. Like his father, he chose to exalt himself instead of letting the Lord to do it.

The book of Daniel records that King Belshazzar held a great banquet for 1,000 nobles, eating and drinking wine with them. With all his inhibitions lifted, he felt invincible, free to say and do whatever he pleased. At some point in the festivities, while Belshazzar was carousing with his cronies, "he gave orders to bring in the gold and silver goblets that Nebuchadnezzar, his father, had taken from the Temple in Jerusalem, so that the king and his nobles, his wives and his concubines might drink from them" (Dan. 5:1–2).

Bad decision. These articles, which were removed from the Temple in Jerusalem during the Israelites' captivity in Babylon, belonged to God. They were consecrated to the Lord for use only in worship. The only people allowed to touch them were Hebrew priests from the tribe of Levi. What Belshazzar failed to remember was that although God shows forgiveness and compassion, He is not one to be trifled with.

GOLD AND SILVER

The servants retrieved the gold goblets and special utensils taken from the Temple in Jerusalem so that the king and his nobles, his wives and his concubines could celebrate and drink from them. They compounded the error by praising the "gods of gold and silver, of bronze, iron, wood and stone" (5:4). Suddenly the fingers of a huge human hand appeared and wrote on the plaster of the wall in the banquet hall. Perhaps the king thought he was either hallucinating or experiencing the after effects of a bad vintage. The king watched the hand as it wrote, and he went pale and wobbly in the knees (5:5–6).

Belshazzar called in all of his trusted advisors to explain the terrifying apparition. When the enchanters, astrologers and diviners arrived at the palace and stood before the agitated monarch, he said, "Whoever reads this writing and tells me what it means will be clothed in purple and have a gold chain placed around his neck, and he will be made the third highest ruler in the kingdom" (5:7).

SUMMONING DANIEL

When no one could read the message or explain what it meant, Belshazzar grew very afraid. The queen knew that Daniel had interpreted dreams and visions for Nebuchadnezzar, and she tried to reassure him. "Don't be alarmed! Don't look so pale! There is a man in your kingdom who has the spirit of the holy gods in him. In the time of your father he was found to have insight and intelligence and wisdom like that of the gods. King Nebuchadnezzar, your father . . . appointed him chief of the magicians, enchanters, astrologers and diviners. This man, Daniel, whom the king called Belteshazzar, was found to have a keen mind and knowledge and understanding, and also the ability to interpret dreams, explain riddles and solve difficult problems. Call for Daniel, and he will tell you what the writing means" (5:10–12).

Daniel was brought before Belshazzar, and the king said, "Now I have heard that you are able to give interpretations and to solve difficult problems. If you can read this writing and tell me what it means, you will be clothed in purple and have a gold chain placed around your neck, and you will be made the third highest ruler in the kingdom" (5:16).

Daniel knew that whatever interpretation he offered had to be one hundred percent honest or that God would work in and through someone else. He also knew that the Lord was not one to suffer fools or to play fast and loose with the deep things of God.

Daniel told the king, "You may keep your gifts for yourself and give your rewards to someone else. But I will read the writing for you and tell you what it means." He reminded him of how Nebuchadnezzar had been humbled before God. "But you his son, O Belshazzar, have not humbled yourself, though you knew all this. Instead, you have set yourself up against the Lord of heaven. You had the goblets from His Temple brought to you, and you and your nobles, your wives and your concubines drank wine from them. You praised the gods of silver and gold, of bronze, iron, wood and stone, which cannot see or hear or understand. But you did not honor the God who holds in His hand your life and all your ways" (5:17, 22–23).

Most people would not have had the nerve to confront an absolute monarch with the power of life and death, as did Daniel. But then again, few quote the Almighty either.

GOD'S MESSAGE

God sent the hand to write this inscription: *MENE, MENE, TEKEL, PARSIN.*

"This is what these words mean: (*Mene*): God has numbered the days of your reign and brought it to an end. (*Tekel*): You have been weighed on the scales and found wanting. (*Peres/Parsin*): Your kingdom is divided and given to the Medes and Persians" (5:26–28).

In spite of this gloomy prediction, Belshazzar was true to his word and rewarded Daniel as promised. He was clothed in a purple robe, given a golden chain of office and elevated to the third highest-ranking position in the kingdom. In most places, the customary practice was to kill the messenger who brought bad news (5:29). But before the night was over, Belshazzar, king of the Babylonians, had died and Darius the Mede took over the kingdom (5:30–31).

A good lesson for all of us to remember—it's not about us—it's about God!

You Can't Take It With You
The Rich Young Ruler

അഇ

J esus told a parable, as recorded in the Gospel of Luke, that sounds
eerily similar to the tales of Nebuchadnezzar and Belshazzar. During
one of His many excursions around the countryside preaching and
teaching, Jesus was asked to settle a probate related question. He used
the opportunity to teach a lesson on greed and ego that both Old Testament kings could have related to quite easily. "Watch out! Be on your
guard against all kinds of greed; a man's life does not consist in the
abundance of his possessions" (Luke 12:15).

The character in Jesus' parable, a wealthy agricultural magnate (aka
farmer), had such a successful crop one year that he thought he needed
extra storage space for the harvest. Unfortunately, like Nebuchadnezzar, he believed that the increase in productivity resulted solely from his
own expertise. He paid almost no tribute to the diligence of his employees, the combination of rainfall and climate, the absence of insect infes-
tation, and political/economic stability, all part of the abundant grace of
the Lord Himself. All he wanted was to have enough money to retire
early, "eat, drink and be merry," party with super models and enjoy a life
of ease and conspicuous consumption (12:19).

BIGGER BARNS

Instead of rejoicing in the Lord's gracious generosity, the landowner
decided to make some major capital improvements on his farm. He

contacted his architect and drew up elaborate plans for new and bigger barns. Within days he had arranged for wrecking crews to come and tear down the old barns and prepare the lot for expansion. But in all this elaborate preparation, he neglected to thank God and to make even the slightest provision for his farm hands. Had he taken steps to secure adequate housing and facilities for his employees, the Lord's judgment might not have fallen quite so harshly.

When the man died suddenly, all of his grandiose building plans went to someone else and he never had a chance to enjoy the blessings of his affluence. God said to him, "You fool! This very night your life will be demanded from you. Then who will get what you have prepared for yourself? This is how it will be with anyone who stores up things for himself but is not rich toward God" (12:20–21).

ACQUISITION

The farmer placed all his confidence in what money could provide—power, influence and possessions—to boost his prestige and social standing. He could have built hospitals and free clinics, helped to end poverty and disease, endowed a school for poor children, and supported countless other projects for people on the margins of society. But, no. He was dead and all the wealth he had so lusted after went to someone else.

The story is told of a miserly billionaire who wanted to take his wealth with him. He demanded that his son and only heir, in order to receive his inheritance, arrange for his father to be buried with 100 million dollars. No millions, no inheritance. After some agonizing deliberation the young heir found a way to fulfill the letter if not the spirit of the request. He arranged for his father to be buried with a check for 100 million. And just to be safe, he called the bank the next day and made sure to stop payment on the check.

Have you noticed that there is never an armored truck following the hearse to the cemetery? You cannot take it with you. Jesus reminded His hearers not to worry about their everyday needs of food, shelter and clothing. Christ said that next to knowing God, serving Him and helping others in His name, everything else was secondary (12:17–21).

We are commanded to "seek His kingdom, and these things will be given to you as well. Sell your possessions and give to the poor. Provide purses for yourselves that will not wear out, a treasure in heaven that will not be exhausted, where no thief comes near and no moth destroys. For where your treasure is, there your heart will be also" (12:31–34). We are to use our resources for the building of the Kingdom of God and His people and joyfully allow the Lord to bless our giving.

This sure eases the stress of trying to be rich—or being known for all time as the rich fool. I am sure you can think of much better ways to be remembered.

Egomania

Haman

⋘⊙⊙⋙

The use of ethnic cleansing and genocide to annihilate rival cultures began not with Hitler during World War II or with oppressive regimes like those found in Bosnia or Sudan. The Bible records an attempt by King Xerxes' chief minister, Haman, to eliminate all Jews held captive in Persia during the exile. Haman sought to be rid of them once and for all by ingratiating himself with the king and purporting to eradicate an enemy of the state. The only problem was that the supposed enemy was not dangerous and certainly not a threat—except to Haman's insatiable longing for power and wealth.

Little did Haman realize that he was dealing with God's chosen people, let alone perceive the possible consequences of his actions. It was a bit like the Chinese proverb Tom Clancy used in one of his techno-thrillers, "you may be able to grab the tiger by the tail, but you had better have a plan about what to do with his teeth at the other end."

Queen Vashti, wife of King Xerxes of Persia, had angered the king after asserting herself by refusing to answer his beck and call. So the royal recruiter, Mordecai, who happened to be Jewish, found a more suitable consort in his cousin Esther, who was also Jewish. The search process was eerily reminiscent of the handsome prince looking for Cinderella, having every female try on the famed glass slipper until he found the one foot that fit perfectly. Esther must have been a real stunner—drop dead gorgeous, with a regal countenance and demeanor that captivated the king right from the start.

ESTHER

"Mordecai had a cousin named Hadassah, whom he had brought up because she had neither father nor mother. This girl, who was also known as Esther, was lovely in form and features, and Mordecai had taken her as his own daughter when her father and mother died. When the king's order and edict had been proclaimed, many girls were brought to the citadel of Susa and put under the care of Hegai. Esther also was taken to the king's palace and entrusted to Hegai, who had charge of the harem. The girl pleased him and won his favor. Immediately he provided her with beauty treatments and special food. He assigned to her seven maids selected from the king's palace and moved her and her maids into the best place in the harem" (Esth. 2:7–10).

As a precaution to ensure Esther's safety, Mordecai had forbidden her to reveal her nationality and family background (2:10). She was such a gorgeous woman, inside and out, that the king favored her above all the other women in his harem and made her queen in Vashti's place with great celebration (2:17).

One day as Mordecai was standing by the palace gate, he overheard a plot by two of the king's officers to assassinate King Xerxes. Mordecai told Esther, who then informed the king of her cousin's discovery. The grateful king was in love with Esther and indebted to Mordecai with an obligation that could not be easily forgotten (2:21–23). He ordered the two conspirators hanged and hailed Mordecai as a hero.

HAMAN

Here the Bible makes an abrupt transition, recording that "After these events, King Xerxes honored Haman, son of Hammedatha, the Agagite, elevating him and giving him a seat of honor higher than that of all the other nobles. All of the royal officials at the king's gate knelt down and paid honor to Haman, for the king had commanded this concerning him" (3:1–2). Mordecai, however, would not kneel or pay homage to Haman, who took it as a personal affront in spite of Mordecai's standing with the king. Meanwhile, some of the king's officials discovered that Mordecai was a Jew and informed Haman (3:3–4).

Haman, enraged by this perceived assault on his ego, didn't want to get angry—he wanted to get even. Not satisfied with retaliating against

Mordecai alone, Haman wanted to systematically exterminate his family, his extended family, his distant family and all of the Jews living in captivity in Persia (3:6).

Haman presented a plan to the king that sounded like he was protecting the empire. He said to King Xerxes, "There is a certain people dispersed and scattered among the peoples in all the provinces of your kingdom whose customs are different from those of all other people and who do not obey the king's laws; it is not in the king's best interest to tolerate them. If it pleases the king, let a decree be issued to destroy them, and I will put 10,000 talents of silver into the royal treasury for the men who carry out this business" (3:8–9).

King Xerxes took his signet ring from his finger and gave it to Haman. "Keep the money and do with the people as you please" (3:10–11). Xerxes then issued an official order to kill all of the Jews—young and old, women and children—on the thirteenth day of the twelfth month, the month of Adar, and to plunder their goods. A copy of the edict, legally binding in every province, was given to people of every nationality so they would be ready when the day arrived (3:13–14).

At that time no judicial review existed to guarantee due process or to ensure the constitutionality of the law. Xerxes was above the law and once he made a decree, it could not be repealed. And what king is going to admit that he was wrong and repeal his own law? Not likely. The order could be superseded or replaced but only by the king himself.

FACING EXTINCTION

Once the edict had been publicized, all the Jews in Persia grew terrified and bewildered. Mordecai and the other Hebrews tore their clothes as a sign of deep anguish, covered themselves in ashes and wailed loudly and bitterly over the imminent death that stared them in the face (4:1, 3). When Queen Esther discovered the real reason behind the extermination edict, she and Mordecai agonized over how to persuade the king to change the law and put an end to Haman's evil plot.

She knew that this would be a difficult task since no one could just waltz into the royal quarters unannounced. Unless first summoned by the king, a person might well be summarily escorted to the dungeon or the executioner's block. Esther realized that once the king discovered that she was a subversive, she would face the same fate as her fellow

Jews. But Mordecai encouraged her to speak for her countrymen by reminding her that it may have been for this situation—to protect the Jews—that she had been born and chosen as queen.

Soon after the decree was issued, the king, still captivated by Esther's charm and grace, saw her at the palace and asked, "What is it, Queen Esther? What is your request? Even up to half the kingdom, it will be given you" (5:3).

Careful not to tip the scales too soon by openly confronting Haman, she responded, "If it pleases the king, let the king, together with Haman, come today to a banquet I have prepared for him" (5:4). While there King Xerxes asked what he could do to please her. Again she said that she would like the king and Haman to attend another state banquet she had prepared and that she would give her answer then.

Haman left the banquet hall with his ego inflated nearly to the point of exploding. He thought he was the most important and indispensable man in the kingdom, perhaps a better candidate for king than even Xerxes. As he left he met Mordecai, who still refused to defer to him, and he became enraged. But he controlled his temper for the moment and went home to share his tale of good fortune with his wife and friends, confident that soon he would be elevated to a position of great wealth and responsibility.

"And that's not all," Haman boasted. "I'm the only person Queen Esther invited to accompany the king to the banquet she gave. And she has invited me along with the king tomorrow. But all this gives me no satisfaction as long as I see that Jew Mordecai sitting at the king's gate" (5:12–13). He just could not enjoy his recognition without making sure that his revenge against Mordecai was complete.

PLOTTING REVENGE

His wife, Zerah, every bit as ambitious as Haman, suggested that to impress the king while ridding himself of his mortal enemy, Haman should "Have a gallows built, 75 feet high, and ask the king in the morning to have Mordecai hanged on it. Then go with the king to the dinner and be happy." Haman loved the idea and had it built that night (5:14).

In the middle of the night, the king could not sleep. Perhaps the sawing and hammering of the gallows project kept him up. So he ordered someone to read the chronicles of his reign to him until he got sleepy. It was no coincidence that the portion being read was about Mordecai's unveiling of the assassination conspiracy (6:1–2).

Realizing he had never truly expressed his gratitude, the king asked, "What honor and recognition has Mordecai received for this?" His attendants replied that nothing had been done.

Just then Haman entered the court fresh from supervising the gallows construction and ready to arrange for Mordecai's execution, not realizing that the king was actually pondering a reward for Mordecai.

The king asked Haman, "What should be done for the man the king delights to honor?" (6:6) In a classic bit of miscommunication, Haman thought the king was making plans to honor him. He answered the king, "For the man the king delights to honor, have them bring a royal robe the king has worn and a horse the king has ridden, one with a royal crest placed on its head. Then let the robe and horse be entrusted to one of the king's most noble princes. Let them robe the man the king delights to honor, and lead him on the horse through the city streets, proclaiming before him, 'This is what is done for the man the king delights to honor!'" (6:7–9).

Beaming with delight, Haman could almost see the victory parade and hear the praise of the cheering crowds, who would be eager to bask in glory with the most powerful man in Persia. The king's next words must have hit Haman like a pole-axed steer at the slaughterhouse. "Go at once," the king commanded Haman. "Get the robe and the horse and do just as you have suggested for Mordecai the Jew, who sits at the king's gate. Do not neglect anything you have recommended" (6:10).

HUMBLE PIE

Tasting the bitterness of humble pie, Haman did as he was told, parading Mordecai around town in his new suit on the king's horse, all the while seething over the honor that he felt rightfully belonged to him. Once the victory parade ended, Haman ran home to share the bad news with his wife. Since Mordecai was Jewish and in favor with the king, Haman was in serious trouble. As the two were lamenting their plight and perhaps searching for a way out, the king's messengers arrived with a limousine chariot to take Haman to Queen Esther's banquet.

At dinner the king reiterated his promise to do whatever pleased the queen. As they sat at the table enjoying the savory dishes and fine wines

(Haman had no doubt lost his appetite by now), Esther dropped the bombshell that Haman had been dreading. "If I have found favor with you, O king, and if it pleases your majesty, grant me my life—this is my petition. And spare my people—this is my request. For I and my people have been sold for destruction and slaughter and annihilation. If we had merely been sold as male and female slaves, I would have kept quiet, because no such distress would justify disturbing the king." (7:3–4).

The king asked, "Who is he? Where is the man who has dared to do such a thing?" (7:5). Without missing a beat, all Esther had to do was gaze across the table with a look that could kill and say, "The adversary and enemy is this vile Haman" (7:6). Haman was terrified. The king stormed off in a rage, and while he was away Haman begged Easter to spare his life. As he did he fell on her on the couch where she was reclining.

At this point the king returned, exclaiming, "Will he even molest the queen while she is with me in the house?" As soon as he said that, his guards roughly shoved a hood over Haman's face, clapped him in irons and hauled him off to the dungeon.

Just then one of the king's attendants chimed in, "A gallows 75 feet high stands by Haman's house. He had it made for Mordecai, who spoke up to help the king" (7:9). The king in his fury said, "Hang him on it!"

SELF-DETERMINATION

The next day King Xerxes took off his signet ring, which he had reclaimed from Haman's corpse, and presented it to Mordecai, while Esther appointed him to rule over Haman's estate. The king then issued a new decree allowing the Jews to arm and defend themselves throughout the Persian Empire. This order effectively gave the Jews the right of self-determination, which they had not enjoyed since being brought into captivity (8:11–14). With Haman's corpse still slowly twisting in the breeze, Mordecai left the palace "wearing royal garments of blue and white, a large crown of gold and a purple robe of fine linen" while the city of Susa held a joyous celebration in his honor (8:15).

Instead of facing a reign of terror throughout the empire, the Jews entered a period of joy, peace and wellbeing. Their enemies, of which Haman had been but one, were now left fearful for their own survival. In fact, the tables were turned as the Jews went on the offensive and defeated those who were once ready to destroy them. Scripture states that no one could stand before them, giving them a military presence not seen since the glory days of kings David and Solomon.

Here, as in other times when His people were in danger, the Lord brought prosperity and protection to them. So if you plan to harm, physically, verbally or emotionally, someone the Lord loves, consider it carefully for it may not be quite as good an idea as you may think.

A Royal Multitasker

King Solomon

ᘓᕥᕤᘔ

King Solomon, the eldest son of David and the last king to rule a
united Israel, has become widely known as the epitome of wisdom
in the Bible. He asked the Lord for wisdom to avoid controversy and political infighting, which had been the Achilles heel of many rulers before
him. God was so impressed with his request for wisdom rather than
wealth, military victory, and solid gold chariots, that he threw in all the
rest of these for good measure.

Solomon had riches beyond description, peace on all fronts, success in everything he attempted and basically, everything he could
have ever wanted, needed or expected. Here is a brief glimpse of his
vast acquisitions:

Solomon accumulated chariots and horses; he had fourteen
hundred chariots and twelve thousand horses, which he kept
in the chariot cities and also with him in Jerusalem. The
king made silver as common in Jerusalem as stones, and
cedar as plentiful as sycamore-fig trees in the foothills.
Solomon's horses were imported from Egypt and from Kue—
the royal merchants purchased them from Kue. They im-
ported a chariot from Egypt for six hundred shekels of silver,
and a horse for a hundred and fifty. They also exported them
to all the kings of the Hittites and of the Arameans (I Kings
10:26–29).

Of course, that doesn't include Solomon's gold and ivory throne, or ornate palaces with gold fixtures. The Temple he built as a spectacular place to worship God was overlaid in pure gold, inside and out.

Although noted for his intelligence, he was a bit sluggish when it came to his family and relationships. People in Solomon's era had no qualms with multiple marriages, but the Lord's plan was the same for Solomon as it was back in the Garden of Eden for Adam and Eve—one man and one woman married to each other for life.

Polygamy had prompted infighting and divided family loyalties among the Hebrew patriarchs, including Abraham, Isaac, Jacob and Solomon's own father, David. Years earlier, the Lord had warned His people not to intermarry with foreigners and allow their gods to dilute true worship and obedience. But it appears that Solomon never met a possession he could not own or a pretty woman he could not make one of his wives. "King Solomon, however, loved many foreign women besides Pharaoh's daughter—Moabites, Ammonites, Edomites, Sidonians and Hittites. They were from nations about which the Lord had told the Israelites, 'You must not intermarry with them, because they will surely turn your hearts after their gods.' Nevertheless, Solomon held fast to them in love. He had *700 wives* of royal birth and *300 concubines*, and his wives led him astray" (I Kings 11:1–3).

TURNING AWAY

Scripture reveals that as Solomon grew older, he allowed his wives to turn his heart away from God. I imagine the last thing Solomon wanted was a confrontation, with so many wives and live-in girl friends. Most men can manage a limited number of essential operations recalling significant dates—spouse's birthday, wedding anniversary and the birthdays of your kids. Imagine trying to accomplish that more than 700 times.

I doubt Solomon could give any of his spouses much time or affection. And as for his kids, Dad's time would be even more limited. How could he teach so many children how to ride a bike, field a ground ball, or fly a kite? What the spouses and children needed was an involved husband and father.

If Solomon was too busy to exert a significant influence in family life when he was young and energetic, things only got worse as he aged. "As Solomon grew old, his wives turned his heart after other gods, and his heart was not fully devoted to the Lord his God, as the heart of David his father had been. He followed Ashtoreth the goddess of the Sidonians, and Molech the detestable god of the Ammonites. So Solomon did evil in the eyes of the Lord; he did not follow the Lord completely, as David his father had done" (I Kings 11:4–6).

Not only did Solomon fail to fulfill his role as a spiritual leader and head of his household, he also abdicated his responsibility to God as the king of Israel. He permitted his wives to worship the idols of their homeland and assisted in building high places of worship for "Chemosh the detestable god of Moab, and for Molech the detestable god of the Ammonites" (11:7–8). Worship of these two foreign deities required the abominable offering of children as human sacrifices.

Solomon had it all—peace, prosperity, wealth beyond description, political stability and the blessing of wisdom. But he lacked the fruit of the spirit to stabilize that wisdom, and he allowed his own desires to override the will of God. Scripture says that twice God appeared to Solomon eager to end his rebellion and sinfulness because "his heart had turned away from the Lord, the God of Israel" (11:9).

Solomon disregarded both of the Lord's warnings, much like we tend to ignore our doctor's advice to change our eating habits and improve our health. Maybe he forgot that everything he had was from God, who gave it freely and could just as easily take it all away. Perhaps he even began to believe that his wisdom was his own. Solomon had been cautioned and given an ultimatum to change his ways. Now he would receive a promise of judgment that would change his life and legacy forever.

The Lord said to Solomon, "Since this is your attitude and you have not kept my covenant and my decrees, which I commanded you, I will most certainly tear the kingdom away from you and give it to one of your subordinates. Nevertheless, for the sake of David your father, I will not do it during your lifetime. I will tear it out of the hand of your son. Yet I will not tear the whole kingdom from him, but will give him one tribe for the sake of David my servant and for the sake of Jerusalem, which I have chosen." (11:11–13). Solomon would not see this happen during his lifetime, and the kingdom would not be handed to a rival family because the Lord still had a special place in His heart for Solomon's father, King David.

ADVERSARIES

Where Solomon once had peace, the Lord "raised up against him an adversary, Hadad the Edomite, from the royal line of Edom," one of the last survivors of a bloody civil war in which his entire family had died (11:14–15). In addition to being an opponent of Solomon, Hadad was closely aligned by marriage to the Pharaoh in Egypt, who became his ally against Israel.

As if that were not enough, the Lord raised up another enemy, "Rezon son of Eliada, who had fled from his master, Hadadezer king of Zobah" (11:23). Rezon gathered a band of young rebels who controlled the area around Damascus to oppose Israel.

Solomon may have given his wives free rein in an effort to keep peace in his family. But in catering to their whims and demands, he missed the opportunity to be a spiritual leader in his own home as well as for the nation. He had his wisdom, his wives, his prosperity, but he lost his chance to be a faithful husband and father. Turning his back on God may have seemed like a good idea at the time, but it pointed Israel down the path of civil war, captivity and enslavement.

A Couple of Phonies
Ananias and Sapphira

လၜၜၜ

Most of the time we try to make a good impression on others by putting our best foot forward. We package our best traits and deeds in order to be perceived as generous, agreeable and truthful. Yet no matter how hard we work to create a positive persona, at some point our true selves are bound to emerge. That was the case with Ananias and his wife, Sapphira, who decided to lie to the Holy Spirit in a vain attempt to appear better than they really were. This poor decision cost them dearly.

Their story, recounted in chapter five of Acts, chronicles the beginning of the Church following Jesus' life, death and resurrection. It signaled that God would accept no less than total transparency from the disciples of this new spirit-driven movement.

SHARING THE WEALTH

In the early days of the Church, Scripture says that, "All the believers were together and had everything in common. Selling their possessions and goods, they gave to anyone as he had need. Every day they continued to meet together in the temple courts. They broke bread in their homes and ate together with glad and sincere hearts, praising God and enjoying the favor of all the people. And the Lord added to their number daily those who were being saved" (Acts 2:44–47).

Believers willingly shared all they had with each other, observing no hierarchy and no division between clergy and laity. When anyone needed food, clothes, money, medicine or housing, they all pitched in and helped each other. Instead of being defined by ownership and possession, they were marked by generosity and harmonious relationships. Worship was not limited to an hour on Sunday morning in a building with hymnals, forms and liturgies. Rather, true worship consisted of each individual focusing on the needs of others for the good of the community.

Although nothing in Scripture decries having wealth or owning property, the early Christians decided that, in the words of Mr. Spock from Star Trek, "the needs of the many outweigh the needs of the few—or the one." For Ananias and Sapphira, however, the needs of one or two superseded the needs of the many, even the need to be honest before God.

The couple sold a piece of property, kept back part of the money and "put the rest at the apostles' feet" (5:1–2). Nothing indicates that they had to give the entire proceeds of the sale to the Church. They could have pledged as little or as much as they chose to the care and maintenance of the Christian community. They could have kept their land, sold it, invested it or donated it without anyone thinking less of them.

THE BIG LIE

Their wrongdoing was in claiming to donate the entire proceeds to the community when indeed they had not. They lied. Still worse, they lied to the Lord, claiming to give Him a gift far more magnanimous than they actually had. They took credit for the money they withheld in the hope of winning public acclaim for their apparent generosity and selfless service.

Peter discovered the truth and confronted Ananias: "Ananias, how is it that Satan has so filled your heart that you have lied to the Holy Spirit and have kept for yourself some of the money you received for the land? Didn't it belong to you before it was sold? And after it was sold, wasn't the money at your disposal? What made you think of doing such a thing? You have not lied to men but to God" (5:3–4). Busted—and Ananias knew it.

As soon as he heard Peter's rebuke, Ananias "fell down and died. And great fear seized all who heard what had happened" (5:5). What an understatement! Was it a heart attack, stroke or some other violent end? Whatever it was, almost as Peter's words were dying away, Ananias may have grasped his chest or his head and died before his body hit the ground. In that same moment were others wondering how they could pretend to make a similar contribution and still keep their money? Or, having already followed suit, did some people fear they would suffer the same fate? Either way, the Lord had their attention. Almost as part of the order of service, some of the young men of the church came and wrapped up Ananias' body, carted him out and buried him—without fanfare, without eulogy, without even a hasty goodbye.

About three hours later Sapphira entered the meeting without knowing the fate of her husband. Perhaps she had a premonition that something bad was going to happen, with Ananias nowhere in sight and her friends checking her out more intently than ever before.

Peter asked her the same question he had asked Ananias. "Tell me, is this the price you and Ananias got for the land?" And, as had her deceased husband, she answered, "Yes," she said, "that is the price" (5:8).

Peter said, "How could you agree to test the Spirit of the Lord? Look! The feet of the men who buried your husband are at the door, and they will carry you out also" (5:9). And just like Ananias, Sapphira dropped stone cold dead right on the spot. She was wrapped up, carried out and buried right next to her husband (5:10).

If you think the witnesses to the first miraculous termination were spooked, Scripture says that "great fear seized the whole church and all who heard about these events." No one dared to join the apostles on their next rounds to perform "many miraculous signs and wonders among the people" (5:11). Nevertheless, with each passing day more and more people came to believe in Jesus Christ and were added to the church. Although they were now living under God's grace and forgiveness as seen through Jesus, rather than the oppressive nature of the old Mosaic Law, God still was not one to be lied to.

And when they passed the offering plate in Ananias and Sapphira's church the next Sunday, everyone gave generously—as if their lives depended on it. Too bad Ananias and Sapphira didn't get the message in time.

GOOD CHOICES—
AND THE PEOPLE WHO MADE THEM

Not everyone in the Bible made bad choices or ruined their lives by their arrogance, stupidity or presumption. Some of the most significant portions of Scripture involve those who decided either to obey God's will, regardless of the cost or consequences, or made what they thought was a good choice and faced the consequences, dire and dismal as they might be.

Here are some of them. Although they are all different, just as our situations are all unique, they involve a deep relationship with God, willing obedience to His leading, and a reward of peace, forgiveness and grace that transcends short-term gratification.

Chatting With God

Enoch

⁓⊙⊙⊙⁓

While on a long drive, my wife was reading the story of Enoch in the book of Genesis when she asked, "How did Enoch know what God expected? Without the law, the patriarchs and prophets, how did he know what was the right thing to do?"

How *did* Enoch know? There was no Scripture until Moses wrote it years later. Without Scripture, there was no law. Without the law, how did people know whether they had broken it? If there was no generally agreed upon code of ethical behavior, how could anyone be held accountable?

Since it would be many generations before the Ten Commandments codified rules of responsible worship and civil cooperation, perhaps revelation came directly from God to the patriarchs. It seems more logical, though, that the Lord's revelation came from the family. Families shared stories that tied actions to consequences, which were told from parent to child over the span of centuries. Every teaching of note was passed down this way. Families today still follow this same pattern— they share stories at Thanksgiving, Christmas, birthdays and other special gatherings, and the family lore improves with each retelling.

FAMILY LORE

Through a simple genealogy of the families in Genesis, we can see that it might have been possible for Enoch to ask his great, great, great,

great grandpa Adam, "What was it like in the Garden when you walked with God in the cool of the day?" Enoch would not have intended to berate Adam for the fall and for bringing sin into the world, but rather to discover the nature of his intimacy with God during a blissful time of innocence. I believe Adam would have taken great delight in answering Enoch's questions. Enoch may not have been the only one to understand the magnitude of what was lost, but he was most likely the only one who knew the incredible value of the friendship he still had with God.

In those early days, Enoch learned from his family. But was family the only thing he had? Did he not also have prayer? Only a few long-lived generations before Enoch, some time after Seth had his son Enosh (Enoch's great, great grandfather), "men began to call on the name of the Lord" (Gen. 4:26). The Bible does not indicate whether men called on God in worship or if it was a desperate cry for help, but Enoch, whose name means "to dedicate or to instruct," sought the Lord's direction and called on Him to change his heart.

Unwilling to perpetuate the family tradition of blame and shame, Enoch concentrated all of his energy on the Lord. Unlike King Solomon, who asked for wisdom to rule Israel and to know right from wrong (I Kings 3), Enoch did not ask for wisdom. I believe he asked for holiness instead. Having grown up with the stories of the Fall and its aftermath, Enoch knew that he did not have the spiritual discipline to change on his own. He understood that he would not be able to learn holiness. Instead, holiness would have to come directly from the grace of God.

Enoch instinctively understood the message echoed in Hebrews 12:14: "Make every effort to live in peace with all men and to be holy; without holiness no one will see the Lord." He wanted to know God, see God, hear God, and have fellowship with God, as two friends of like mind and heart. The Lord honored Enoch's request for holiness to such a degree that he was able to look on God's glory and survive.

TAKEN AWAY

Scripture says that Enoch "walked with God," side by side and in deep conversation. The Bible later states that Enoch did not die, at least as we know or experience it. To a cynic it would appear that Enoch vanished one day and was never found. But wouldn't someone have found his remains or some clue as to his whereabouts? The simplest explanation is that the Lord and Enoch went walking and talking, discussing life, eternity and creation, until they had gone so far that it was just too late and too far for Enoch to return. God may have suggested that Enoch might as well come home with Him and continue the conversation uninterrupted—"Enoch walked with God; then he was no more, because God took him away" (Gen. 5:24). In the roll call of the heroes of faith, we read: "By faith Enoch was taken from this life, so that he did not experience death; he could not be found, because God had taken him away. For before he was taken, he was commended as one who pleased God" (Heb. 11:5–6). What a way to go!

The next verse in Hebrews affirms our need to be like Enoch if we are to please God and experience the Lord's favor: "Without faith it is impossible to please God, because anyone who comes to Him must believe that He exists and that He rewards those who earnestly seek Him." This is wise counsel for all who would break free from classic patterns of sin, failure and frustration.

When analyzed in its broadest terms, Scripture can be distilled into a few basic themes—righteousness is rewarded, evil is punished, and we are meant to live in harmony with God. All of the Bible points us to God, helps us reestablish a love relationship with Him, through grace, that was broken in Eden, and guides our life with Him once we know Him as Lord.

From the story of Enoch we learn two things. First, we need to interact with previous generations, to hear the accounts of their personal history and to profit from their wisdom. We need to hear our grandparents share embarrassing stories of our parents' exploits as children so that we can see them as normal people who made some of the same mistakes we did.

Second, we maintain our connection to God by way of conversation with Him—through our behaviors and our prayers. Always abundantly patient, God delights in fulfilling the needs of His people. He longs to hear our prayers. "While we are still speaking," He hears us and is sending the answer along (Isa. 65:24). Sometimes His answer is yes—God gives us what we have asked for. At other times, however, His answer is no—either what we want is not in His plan, or we are not living according to His will. Sometimes the no is more of a not yet, meaning don't give up. But we must keep praying until something changes—the request, the circumstance, or us. The Bible gives us some instruction, for James reminds us, "You do not have, because you do not ask God" (James 4:2). The Lord will answer our requests and questions if we ask Him. I sure would like to live and die like Enoch. Talk about a grand exit!

Going With the Flow
Noah

಄ೋ௸

U nfortunately for the human race, neither Enoch's children nor any of his other descendents inherited his intense longing for holiness. In fact, things only worsened as people experimented with sin in all its combinations and permutations. Like a malevolent virus, sin poisoned every aspect of life and society—a situation not so different from ours today. In an effort to ensure that truth and righteousness would survive, the Lord decided to combat the pervasive nature of sin with water—lots of water—and the help of a righteous man named Noah.

Although much in Scripture is written about the fallen condition of mankind, there is little describing the actual flood or the interaction of Noah's family—the one saved community of believers. From the perspective of the family, the book of Genesis begins with Adam and Eve. The faith community grows as children are born and new generations are added, until ten generations later, it is again reduced to a family unit. Back to square one, you might say. Chapter 6 of Genesis introduces the scene by describing what demographers might call a "population growth trend." But as families grew in numbers, so did their capacity for rebellion.

OUT OF CONTROL

When men began to increase in number on the earth and daughters were born to them, the sons of God saw that the daughters of men were beautiful, and they married any of them they chose. Then the Lord said, "My Spirit will not contend with man forever, for he is mortal; his days will be 120 years." The Nephilim were on the earth in those days—and also afterward—when the sons of God went to the daughters of men and had children by them (Gen. 6:1–4).

Some believe that the Nephilim were pagans, like the giant-sized sons of Anak seen by Moses' spies on their reconnaissance mission into Canaan (Num. 13:26–33). Some think Goliath was one of the Nephilim. All agree that these people, vicious and predatory sinners, cared nothing for the things of God. God saw that "every inclination of the thoughts of the heart [of mankind] was only evil all the time" (6:5).

God's comment, "My Spirit will not contend with man forever" (6:3), indicates just how disappointing mankind had become and how weary the Lord was of the world's sin. His great love project was broken almost beyond repair. So what was He to do? The Lord was going to erase all that He had so joyfully made in the first place: "I will wipe mankind, whom I have created, from the face of the earth—men and animals, and creatures that move along the ground, and birds of the air—for I am grieved that I have made them" (6:7).

But if God can make the world, why can't He just remake it? Recreating everything would be no harder for God than erasing a blackboard and writing on it again. A righteous God, however, must make sure He is fair and just in all things. He leaves no room for "collateral damage" as He executes judgment while protecting the righteous who might get caught in the crossfire.

Should God's act of destroying everything be construed as no more than a petulant fit of anger? Hardly. Only His abundant patience kept the entire human race from obliteration, since it is always the Lord's way to save a righteous remnant from harm while dealing with the guilty. So, despite His regret at having made man in the first place, God provided for a second chance.

GOD'S ORDERS

As the Lord searched the hearts of men, He found Noah "a righteous man, blameless among the people of his time . . . God said to Noah, 'I am going to put an end to all people . . . and the earth. So make yourself an ark of cypress wood; make rooms in it and coat it with pitch inside and out'" (6:9; 13–14).

The word "ark", which appears several times in the Bible, always refers to a vehicle of deliverance: 1) for the human race and animal kingdom 2) an ark of reeds to deliver Moses from Pharaoh's death decree; and 3) as a temple, the Ark of the Covenant, a chest made of acacia wood, overlaid with pure gold to save the hearts and souls of a people called to be holy.

Noah's vessel was to be 450 feet long, 75 feet wide, and 45 feet high, with three distinct levels or decks. God called for a finished roof and side bulkheads that came to 18 inches from the top of the superstructure for light and ventilation. The door would be in the side rather than on the top deck for ease of entry of cargo, supplies, and passengers (6:15–16). Noah must have felt a bit overwhelmed wondering how to construct such a monstrous backyard project, but Scripture describes it as a concept drawing, not a blueprint. The Lord may have added more specific instructions as the project developed—mitered corners, mortise and tenon joints, pegs instead of deck screws—to create an engineering marvel roughly half the size of the Titanic. Since the ark was not steerable and had no means of propulsion, it was more like a floating barn than a boat, traveling where the winds and currents carried it. (Perhaps this is the first use of the phrase "going with the flow").

The Lord went on to explain: "I am going to bring floodwaters on the earth to destroy all life under the heavens, every creature that has the breath of life in it. Everything on earth will perish, but I will establish my covenant with you, and you will enter the ark—you and your sons and your wife and your sons' wives with you" (6:17–18). Noah must have sighed with relief when the Lord finally revealed that his family would be saved. God was very specific, however, in His guest list for this "second chance cruise," with everyone outside of Noah's immediate family subject to punishment. Noah would need all his resolve to shut the door and bar it quickly once the floods came and friends and neighbors began pounding on the hull.

FAITH AND OBEDIENCE

Noah went right to work building the ark and making all the necessary preparations. God specified how many of each kind of animal to take, along with enough food for the animals and human passengers. If any animals perished during the voyage, replacements were at hand (6:19–20; 7:2, 3). Noah did all that the Lord ordered and completed the work when he was 600 years old. (Please bear in mind that it wasn't God's plan for people to die, so they lived hundreds of years in the beginning, while the post-flood limits were set at 120 years of age.) According to Genesis 7:10, the waters came seven days after the ark was loaded, safe and secure with the hatches battened down.

As Noah's crew prepared for this ominous event, they reflected on the Lord's promises. They obeyed God with a willing spirit, in spite of bruises, cuts, and hammered thumbs. While enduring the difficult journey, they lived and worked in a spirit of obedience and faith. For instruction and encouragement, they had the Lord, and to share their needs, concerns, victories, and failures, they had family. Worship was not a ritual or a Sunday morning habit. Worship was life, with God at the center.

On the seventeenth day of the second month, all the springs of the great deep burst forth, and the floodgates of the heavens were opened. Rain fell on the earth for 40 days and 40 nights (7:11–12).

So where did all the water come from? Geological and archaeological studies show that massive seismic activity could have caused unprecedented flooding. If huge underground rivers, lakes, and "springs of the deep" were released, and then storms generated more rain, the water level could have risen to epic proportions. Rainfall at 36 inches per hour would send the average person swimming after only two hours— and keep them swimming for another 958 hours without stopping! Even the Navy Seals would have found it impossible to survive.

By the time of the flood, Methuselah and Lamech were dead, as were most of Noah's direct ancestors. But others who ridiculed Noah and his faith in God pleaded desperately for rescue as the waters crept higher and higher. Did Noah and his family sing songs of praise to God to buoy their faith or to drown out the din of the rain and the wails of those who were drowning? The thankful family kept busy, no doubt, as they rode out God's "perfect storm." Animals had to be fed, cows milked, and lots of hay changed in the stalls so the smell would not be overwhelming!

DRY LAND

With the residents of God's floating menagerie safely tucked in bed, "every living thing on the face of the earth was wiped out . . . Only Noah was left, and those with him in the ark. The waters flooded the earth for 150 days" (7:23–24). Five months into the voyage, did Noah and company think God had forgotten them in their maritime farm? Not for a moment. He stopped the rains and plugged up the springs and sent a powerful wind to begin to dry up the water. After bobbing around for what seemed like an eternity, the ark came to a grinding halt on the mountains of Ararat in what is now Turkey.

It would still take some time before the ground dried enough for the ark's inhabitants to see land (8:4–5), but each new day brought encouragement that the flood was subsiding. Noah and his family had to be patient and wait on God. Patience, however, is something human beings historically have had in short supply. We know what we want, at least we think we do, and we want it now. We want our desires met as quickly as possible, and we especially hate to wait on the Lord, although that is exactly what He expects us to do to demonstrate obedience and faith.

The entire process from flood to finale took 375 days—just over a year. Shortly after Noah's 601st birthday, the water was gone, and everyone disembarked to begin their new lives. They unloaded the animals—or rather opened the door and got out of the way. Were Noah's boys assigned the task of cleaning up after the animals were gone? Did the family live in the ark, trailer-park style, until they could build a more permanent dwelling? Once they stretched their legs and rolled in the grass for the first time in over a year, Noah took some of the animals and sacrificed them to God in worship and thanksgiving. With the old stories about Cain and Abel still fresh in his mind, he respectfully offered the sacrifice in thanksgiving to God for the chance to restart the human race. As the smoke of the sacrifice wafted upward, the Lord saw Noah's heartfelt obedience, and He was pleased, further renewing His promise to "never again . . . destroy all living creatures, as I have done" (8:21).

God blessed Noah's family and again ordered them to "be fruitful and increase in number" (9:1). Every kind of food was given to them, just as with Adam and Eve—except that they were not to eat meat with blood still in it. God was reminding them of the fact that life is in blood, that life is precious, and that God would not tolerate another Cain-and-Abel episode. If anyone took the life of another person, God would demand an accounting. Not only was this decree necessary for civil rule, but also to demonstrate the extraordinary value that man needed to place on human life, which had been created in the "image of God" (9:5–6).

THE RAINBOW COVENANT

By the way, how long can you tread water? Not to worry, for the Lord established a covenant with Noah and all his descendants, bestowing the rainbow as a sign of His pledge never to destroy the world by flood again (9:12–16). And, if you think you are too old or too insignificant to make a difference for the Lord, take heart in this on-line quote: "Remember, the ark was built by a lone amateur. The Titanic was built by a whole bunch of experts."

Read My Lips

Joshua

⌘

Joshua, Moses' confidant during the Exodus, who brought Israel into the Promised Land and led the miraculous siege of Jericho, is one of the few characters in the Bible portrayed without any major flaws. Even Bible greats such as Moses, David and Solomon had plenty of skeletons in their closets, indicating a pattern of disobedience and weakness of character. But not Joshua. He was willing to carry out God's plan when the Lord needed him most.

Joshua, God's personally chosen successor to Moses, took Moses' place after Moses had struck the rock—instead of speaking to it as God ordered—to obtain drinking water for the people. Deuteronomy 34:9 records that he was "full of the spirit of wisdom, because Moses had laid his hands on him; and the Israelites listened to him." Joshua faithfully followed God's command to help Israel drive out the other nations who were living in Canaan. Many Israelites hesitated to trust God fully and quickly developed a policy of semi-peaceful coexistence with their pagan neighbors. But Joshua, who trained for 40 years under Moses' tutelage, did exactly as the Lord, his commander-in-chief, instructed him. He ushered the nation of former slaves into their homeland to enjoy a new period of prosperity and security.

REMEMBERING

Now that the people had settled into their new home, Joshua was ready to retire from public life, having done everything God had ever

asked of him. He called everyone together to impart his spiritual legacy
and to avoid any confusion about what the Lord wanted to accomplish.
Joshua assembled all of the people from the oldest to the youngest and
reminded them of the Lord's deeds on their behalf.

Selective amnesia is a flaw common to all of us—we tend to forget
the blessings we have received, and we always want to know "what has
God done for me lately." Joshua reminded the Hebrews that the Lord
had brought them out of Israel, rescued them from slavery in Egypt, and
then helped them defeat their enemies in Canaan. He told them that God
had given them an inheritance, property they could call their own, and
houses they did not have to build. They harvested crops they had not
planted and received God's support as they continued to reclaim the
land (Josh. 23:3–5).

Joshua's "state of the union" address, although filled with good news
of bright hope, also warned that the chosen people's relationship with
God could not be negotiated. He challenged them to:

> *Be very strong; be careful to obey all that is written in the
> Book of the Law of Moses, without turning aside to the right
> or to the left. Do not associate with these nations that remain
> among you; do not invoke the names of their gods or swear by
> them. You must not serve them or bow down to them. But you
> are to hold fast to the Lord your God, as you have until now.*
>
> *The Lord has driven out before you great and powerful na-
> tions; to this day no one has been able to withstand you. One
> of you routs a thousand, because the Lord your God fights for
> you, just as He promised. So be very careful to love the Lord
> your God.*
>
> *But if you turn away and ally yourselves with the survivors
> of these nations that remain among you and if you inter-
> marry with them and associate with them, then you may be
> sure that the Lord your God will no longer drive out these na-
> tions before you. Instead, they will become snares and traps
> for you, whips on your backs and thorns in your eyes, until
> you perish from this good land, which the Lord your God has
> given you* (23:6–13).

REALITY CHECK

Joshua recalled that throughout their history the Lord had never failed to protect and sustain the Hebrew people. He frequently reiterated that their home was a gift from God, not something they deserved or had earned through their own efforts. He also shared the bad news as well.

> *But just as every good promise of the Lord your God has come true, so the Lord will bring on you all the evil He has threatened, until He has destroyed you from this good land He has given you. If you violate the covenant of the Lord your God, which He commanded you, and go and serve other gods and bow down to them, the Lord's anger will burn against you, and you will quickly perish from the good land He has given you* (23:15–16).

When the twelve tribes gathered together at Shechem, Joshua summoned all of the leaders, elders and other influential people. With the dangers of the Exodus behind them, he recapped the story of Abraham and his departure from Ur in Chaldea, the legacies of Isaac and Jacob, and Moses' success in leading the escape from Pharaoh and slavery. Finally, he recounted the battles with all the "ites"—the Amorites, Perizzites, Canaanites, Hittites, Girgashites, Hivites and Jebusites—to secure their current homeland (24:1–13).

Since there were few books and scrolls available, important information needed to be passed on orally. Joshua reminded the people to "fear the Lord and serve Him with all faithfulness. Throw away the gods your forefathers worshipped beyond the River and in Egypt, and serve the Lord" (24:14). He was referring to the foreign gods the Hebrews had worshipped while enslaved and during their journey to Canaan.

AN ULTIMATUM

Then Joshua gave them an ultimatum along with a promise to obey God as their leader. "But if serving the Lord seems undesirable to you, then choose for yourselves this day whom you will serve, whether the gods your forefathers served beyond the River, or the gods of the Amorites, in whose land you are living. But as for me and my household, we will serve the Lord" (24:15).

Almost unanimously, the people pledged their undying allegiance to the Lord, recalling times when God had defended them and upheld them in the midst of tremendous odds and danger. "We too will serve the Lord, because he is our God" (24:16–18). Joshua, however, knew them better than they knew themselves, recalling the behavior of their ancestors prior to the Exodus, through the Golden Calf fiasco at Sinai, wandering in the desert and up until the present. Knowing their propensity for doing the wrong thing despite their best intentions, Joshua told the people, "You are not able to serve the Lord. He is a holy God; He is a jealous God. He will not forgive your rebellion and your sins. If you forsake the Lord and serve foreign gods, He will turn and bring disaster on you and make an end of you, after He has been good to you" (24:19–21).

The Hebrews cheered all the louder, declaring their enduring loyalty and obedience to God alone. But Joshua reminded them that they were binding themselves to the Lord willingly, and if there were consequences, they would bear the responsibility for breaking the covenant relationship.

The people said to Joshua, "We will serve the Lord our God and obey Him" (24:24).

They forgot the past, but Joshua didn't. Only he and Caleb still remained from the Golden Calf incident and the years in the wilderness.

By the grace of God, the life of holiness modeled by Joshua greatly influenced his family and the nation of Israel. Generations later, many Israelites would forget to be trusting and obedient, but not those who remembered his challenge—"for me and my household, we will serve the Lord." Saying yes to God and granting him first priority in our lives is an excellent choice, and one we would do well to heed ourselves.

Swallowing His Pride

Naaman

ॐ

Sometimes the Lord grants miracles to people we wish He would not bless at all. Whereas we might say, "Let him suffer. It will teach him a lesson," God says, "I'll forgive and heal him. That will teach everyone a lesson." Such was the case with Naaman—the general-in-chief to the king of Aram, a longtime foe of Israel.

As a famous military commander, Naaman was used to getting things done in his way and in his time. Junior officers jumped when he barked orders and career soldiers panicked when he arrived to inspect the troops. Officers and enlisted personnel alike understood that Naaman issued orders, not suggestions, which were to be obeyed immediately, without question or hesitation. A fearless leader on the battlefield, he expected nothing less from his soldiers. He also suffered from one of the most debilitating diseases of his day—leprosy (II Kings 5:1).

A NEAR-DEATH SENTENCE

Cases of leprosy still exist around the world today, usually in developing countries where the standard of medical care is especially deficient. But unlike ancient times when the diagnosis was a near death sentence, today the disease can be arrested and even reversed. In biblical times ignorance and fear engendered social isolation for anyone who contracted leprosy. People afflicted with this illness were removed from the community and relegated to trash dumps outside the city walls.

Leprosy is caused by a bacterial infection that kills nerve cells in the skin and eyes and destroys the sense of touch. A person with leprosy feels no pain and has no reflex reaction to it. In the normally reactive person, a small pebble in the shoe causes extreme discomfort. For someone with leprosy, the pebble creates a blister, then a lesion and finally an infection with severe tissue damage, causing the disfigurement we have come to associate with the disease.

Many people become blind due to nerve damage to the surface of the eye. Since the eye senses no pain and lacks the blink reflex to moisten the surface of the cornea, the sun's rays can cause irreversible blindness. Victims of leprosy cannot feel the firm handshake of a friend, the loving caress of a spouse or the playful hug of an adoring child. They cannot respond either to the cool of a summer breeze or the searing heat of the midday sun.

Naaman's army had just returned victorious, after one of many campaigns against Israel, with trophies, wealth and slaves. One of these slaves was a young girl who worked as a maid for Naaman's wife. Although she could have been bitter and resentful at being forced from her home and family, she felt compassion for Naaman. "If only my master would see the prophet who is in Samaria! He would cure him of his leprosy," she said (5:3). She could have hoarded that information and allowed the enemy of her country to die a slow and agonizing death, far from the care of the people he loved. Instead, she put Naaman's needs first and willingly offered him a practical solution to his problem.

Rather than dismiss her advice because of her gender and lowly position, Naaman took it to heart and went to see the king of Aram. The king said, "By all means, go . . . I will send a letter to the king of Israel" (5:4). In order to open the right doors, Naaman took along ten talents of silver, 6,000 shekels of gold and ten sets of clothing to sweeten the deal (5:5).

THE KING'S LETTER

The king's letter of introduction read: ". . . I am sending my servant Naaman to you so that you may cure him of his leprosy" (5:6). But the king of Israel was furious. As soon as he read the letter, he tore his robes and said, "Am I God? Can I kill and bring back to life? Why does this fel-

low send someone to me to be cured of his leprosy? See how he is trying to pick a quarrel with me!" (5:7). He knew he was powerless to cure
such a mysterious and malevolent malady.

Fortunately Elisha heard about Naaman's plight and freely offered
his assistance so that he might glorify God. "Have the man come to me
and he will know that there is a prophet in Israel" (5:8).

Buoyed by the news, Naaman traveled to Elisha's house with an en-
tourage of horses and chariots in order to make a suitable impression.
Elisha, on the other hand, treated Naaman's visit like another day at the
office. In fact, he didn't even go out to meet the general; he sent a messenger to deliver the news. Elisha was sending a private to deliver a
message that should have been delivered by at least a regimental commander. He wasn't trying to humiliate Naaman; it was just that Elisha
knew who had the real power—God, not Naaman.

The messenger said, "Go, wash yourself seven times in the Jordan,
and your flesh will be restored and you will be cleansed" (5:10). This
was phase one in Naaman's healing process. His prideful arrogance had
to be broken before his body could be healed. Naaman was a proud
man—proud of his country, his wealth and his influence, and he needed
to know and acknowledge that God was truly in charge of his life.

Naaman was irate, to say the least. "I thought that he would surely
come out to me and stand and call on the name of the Lord his God,
wave his hand over the spot and cure me of my leprosy. Are not Baan
and Harper, the rivers of Damascus, better than any of the waters of Israel? Couldn't I wash in them and be cleansed?" (5:11–12).

The general expected a magical cure because of his position and reputation. If he had to earn his healing, he would gladly have invaded a
city or led a major campaign against one of Israel's enemies. But just the
thought of washing himself in one of Israel's muddy, second rate rivers
made him nauseous. Can you imagine the Queen of England being instructed to wash in the Thames, rather than in water especially pumped
in for use at Buckingham Palace?

Fortunately, Naaman's servants had more sense than their master, for
they begged him to stop complaining and obey Elisha. If Elisha had told
Naaman to do a great deed, he would have done it without question.
How much more, then, should he swallow his pride and go and do as he
was told. He was a man under orders, albeit a man used to giving orders
rather than taking them.

SEVEN BATHS

Naaman eventually humbled himself, went to the Jordan River and bathed. He did it once, twice, three times, always checking to see if there was some change in his condition. He went back four, five, six times—still no change. On the seventh trip to the river, as he toweled off and began to change back into his armor, he felt a tingling sensation all over his body and noticed that the scaly white patches of infection and decay had been replaced with soft, pink skin like that of a baby (5:14).

"It worked! That crazy old prophet was right," he must have shouted gleefully, running back to show everyone that he had been healed. Amazing how the Lord was willing to help even a potential enemy of Israel in order to show His power and glory. But isn't that just like our God to be inclusive to all who seek His grace and mercy?

Naaman was so thrilled that he and his aide ran back to Elisha to share the good news. In a true moment of epiphany, he told Elisha, "Now I know that there is no God in all the world except in Israel. Please accept now a gift from your servant" (5:15). Yet as many times as Naaman tried to leave some form of payment to show his gratitude, Elisha refused. Elisha knew the miracle was of God and that He alone was worthy of any thanks or praise. Naaman promised never to offer sacrifices to any deity other than the Lord Almighty (5:16–17). In an interesting footnote to this story, he told Elisha that one of his duties was to escort the king into the temple of the pagan god Rimmon and then bow down to this idol with his master. When he asked for forgiveness for this offense against the Lord, Elisha replied, "Go in peace." Elisha must have known that God would honor the purity of Naaman's heart and have mercy on his predicament.

After Naaman left to go home, Elisha's servant, Gehazi, decided to take advantage of his generosity. Sure, it was fine for the old prophet to rely on God for everything, he thought. But what can I, a mere servant, count on for a pension, investments or financial security? If Elisha doesn't want the things Naaman brought, I do. With that he ran to catch up with the general.

When Naaman looked in the rearview mirror of his chariot and saw Gehazi running to catch up, he stopped and asked if there was a problem. "Everything is all right," Gehazi answered. "My master sent me to say, 'Two young men from the company of the prophets have just come

to me from the hill country of Ephraim. Please give them a talent of silver and two sets of clothing'" (5:21). Elisha, of course, had never said
any such thing.

An unsuspecting Naaman gladly gave Gehazi everything he asked for
and even sent two servants to help him transport the goods. Gehazi carried the booty the last few miles himself so that he could hide it in his
house.

ERRAND OF GREED

Fresh from his errand of greed, he reported to Elisha as if nothing
had happened. "Where have you been, Gehazi?" Elisha asked.

"Your servant didn't go anywhere," Gehazi lied (5:25).

Did Gehazi really think he could pull a fast one on a man who speaks
for God and does miracles? Elisha knew what had happened just as if
he had been there. "Was not my spirit with you when the man got down
from his chariot to meet you? Is this the time to take money, or to accept clothes, olive groves, vineyards, flocks, herds, or menservants and
maidservants?" Rather than let such deception go unpunished, he
added, "Naaman's leprosy will cling to you and to your descendants forever." Gehazi then departed from Elisha's presence to face the fate that
had once been Naaman's.

Naaman, stirred by need and humbled before God, was restored,
healed and given a second chance. But that is how the Lord's grace and
forgiveness works. Without being humbled and made aware of our inability to change ourselves, none of us can know the cleansing power of
forgiveness. If we think we deserve it, we'll never know the meaning of
grace.

"Go See This Thing Now!"

The Bethlehem Shepherds

During the course of a lifetime, we sometimes tend to lose the wonder, mystery and excitement of Christmas as we become overly familiar with the story. Because we know what to expect, we don't try to discover anything new or exciting. Yet the anticipation of the arrival of the Messiah was what gave people hope for thousands of years.

Perhaps that is why what Luke does not record in the Christmas story seems almost as fascinating as what he does reveal. We know that the shepherds made one of the world's greatest decisions in running to Bethlehem and finding the baby Jesus. I just wonder what happened to these ordinary men after they returned home. Sometimes choices, even good ones, come with consequences.

We know that the shepherds "in the fields nearby, keeping watch over their flocks at night" (Luke 2:8) were the first to hear the announcement of the Savior's birth. In the middle of a long, dreary night of caring for the sheep, an angel in gleaming white appeared to them and said, "Do not be afraid. I bring you good news of great joy that will be for all the people. Today in the town of David a Savior has been born to you; He is Christ the Lord. This will be a sign to you: You will find a baby wrapped in cloths and lying in a manger." (2:10–12). At the revelation of such incredible news, the whole sky exploded in light as an angelic choir sang "Glory to God in the highest, and on earth peace to men on whom His favor rests" (2:14).

RUNNING TO SEE JESUS

Many people, after regaining their emotional equilibrium, might have been content to enjoy the celestial concert and let it go at that. But the shepherds obediently decided to travel to Bethlehem and see this glorious event without discussing the pros and cons or even requesting a day off from work. Their only choice was to leave the sheep unattended while they ran to see the Messiah-child. They leapt headlong into God's unknown adventure, trusting Him for the outcome.

In Luke 2:16–18 the Bible records that the shepherds ran and found everything just as the angel had said. "The shepherds returned, glorifying and praising God for all the things they had heard and seen, which were just as they had been told" (2:20).

But is that all? The following story captures what might have happened as a result of the shepherds' journey to Bethlehem 2,000 years ago.

****

While the shepherds were away, temple guards came to inspect the sheep that would be sold as sacrifices on Holy Days to cover the sins of the people. They found the sheep unattended, except for a strange young man dressed in gleaming white. Without being given a chance to explain, the shepherds were arrested and hauled off to the Temple brig, charged with multiple counts of absence without leave, dereliction of duty, insubordination and failure to obey a direct order.

If convicted at a court-martial, the shepherds would have faced termination with a dishonorable discharge, confinement, a hefty fine and loss of pay and benefits. Perhaps the court-martial might have gone something like this.

THE TRIAL

Prosecution: "We acknowledge that the shepherds have done a good job tending the Temple sheep. But past history in no way excuses their leaving the flock subject to theft, injury and predators. To leave them in the care of another, regardless of the alleged angelic affiliation, is nothing less than gross negligence and culpable dereliction of duty."

The prosecution called a host of witnesses who had seen the shepherds in Bethlehem when they should have been on duty in the hills outside of town. All the prosecution had to do to win the case was establish that the shepherds had deserted their posts without permission, thus disobeying a direct order never to leave the sheep alone.

Prosecution: "Did you leave your posts to go to Bethlehem?"
Shepherds: "Yes."
Prosecution: "Did you have permission?"
Shepherds: "No, we did not."
Prosecution: "Were you previously ordered to stay until relieved?"
Shepherds: "Yes, we were."
Prosecution: "Did you leave without such permission?"
Shepherds: "Yes sir, we did."
Prosecution: "Your honor, the prosecution rests. By their own admission they left the sheep unprotected and without permission."

THE DEFENSE

The defense then put the shepherds on the stand to share their perspective on what happened in Bethlehem that night.

Defense: "Would you tell the court in your own words why you left the sheep?"
Shepherds: "The angel said to."

The prosecutor jumped to his feet. "Objection, your honor. Does the defense expect the court to believe that common shepherds converse with angels?" You could hear the sarcasm dripping off each word. "Relevance?"

Judge: "Overruled."
Shepherds: "There were actually thousands of them, and one told us of the Messiah being born in Bethlehem in a stable. It was just as he said."
Prosecution: "Objection—hearsay. Move to strike."
Judge: "Overruled. Sit down and keep quiet. I want to hear what they have to say."
Defense: "Did you see the Child?"

Shepherds: "Yes sir, we did."

Defense: "Did he perform some sort of miracle?"

Shepherds: "No."

Defense: "Did he or his parents look in any way royal or especially gifted?"

Prosecution: "Your honor, I most strenuously object. This requires a conclusion on the part of the witnesses. God in a stable? Your honor, move to strike the last testimony."

Judge: "Overruled. For the last time, sit down and be quiet or you will find yourself in contempt of court!"

Shepherds: "Your honor, there was nothing unusual about them except they seemed so kind and caring. They had an inner sense of purpose. We can't describe it. It just felt like we were on holy ground. Powerful, yet serene."

Defense: "Do you have anything else to add in your own defense?"

Shepherds: "No, except for the song the angels sang. They taught it to us."

The shepherds then launched into a four-part harmony of "Glory to God in the highest!" After they finished singing to the hushed courtroom, the judge dismissed the jury to deliberate and reach a verdict.

The deliberations were short—a sign the prosecution took to indicate that the shepherds would soon be on their way to the brig for a long time, ending all this foolishness about angels and Messiah-babies once and for all.

The panel silently filed back into the courtroom, ready to render their verdict.

THE VERDICT

Judge: "The accused will stand with counsel. The panel may publish the verdict."

Foreman: "On all charges and specifications we find the shepherds— guilty. However, they were guilty only of a violation of man's law and the expectations of their employers. They were in full compliance with orders from an angel, who served as an official representative of God to help complete a very old prophecy. They were also in accord with the plan of God to proclaim the 'good news of great joy' as commanded. For that reason, there will be no punishment of any kind.

"Furthermore, we'd like to thank them for their wholehearted and enthusiastic proclamation. And if they have time, we would like them to tell us in great detail all that happened concerning the arrival of the Messiah—and maybe teach us the angels' song too!"

With a resounding ring of the gavel, the judge declared, "This ends the case against the Bethlehem shepherds. Court is adjourned!"

Sometimes a person needs to respond to the things of God and trust the consequences and results to Him. The shepherds had been in the presence of the Eternal and everyone knew it, for nothing could stop them from talking about all they had seen and heard.

The same good news of grace and forgiveness is for us, too, as the Lord creates in us the holy nature and character of God. Take the message of Christ personally. Come to Him—and come running—just like the shepherds. Hey, we can always find you a good lawyer.

"You Want Us to Do What?"

The Twelve Disciples

⌒◈◈⌒

At times we respond to available opportunities without hesitation. In other cases we like to take our time to ensure fiscally sound choices that will bolster our life goals. While we may jump at the chance for an impulse purchase on the television-shopping network, we like to move slowly with life-changing decisions that involve career, re-location and financial security. Even though we may be quite taken with a certain house, we usually shop for the best financing and authorize an inspection to uncover hidden problems long before we sign on the dotted line. Sometimes we treat a potential spouse with intense scrutiny, yet it is possible for near strangers to find fulfillment in many happy years of marriage.

With anything that involves a sizable investment or risk in terms of money, emotion or commitment, we want to cover all the bases. Yet Jesus' first disciples, a rag tag band of misfits and antagonists, chose to follow Him immediately, irrevocably changing their lives and their contribution to history forever.

FIRST CENTURY RABBIS

In first century Israel young Jewish males had to apply for apprenticeship to a rabbi, much like a prospective student would apply to a university today. They engaged in a highly competitive process, and only a small percentage from the top tier of applicants managed to make the final cut. So in choosing twelve ordinary, uneducated men to be his disciples, Jesus turned the religious order upside down. It was a rare honor to be personally chosen to follow a rabbi in Galilee, which helps explain why all of the disciples immediately dropped everything to follow in the footsteps of the Master. In John 15:16 Jesus reminds the Twelve of his unique relationship with them as He prepares them for his death and the coming of the Holy Spirit. "You did not choose me, but I chose you and appointed you to go and bear fruit—fruit that will last."

Matthew's gospel records Jesus walking beside the Sea of Galilee fairly early in His ministry, watching several local fishermen plying their trade and casting their nets into the large inland lake. As he passed by He saw two brothers "Simon called Peter and his brother Andrew" fishing there. Without any apparent preamble, Jesus said, "Come, follow me, and I will make you fishers of men" (Matt. 4:18–19). He didn't promise them an office with a view, a company car, a six-figure salary, a pension, health insurance or any other perks that a headhunter might use to entice a prospective employee.

Peter and Andrew were not recreational fishermen out for a relaxing afternoon, trying to catch a few fish for supper. They were commercial fishermen with employees, assets and all the other obligations of a successful business—boats, nets, storage buildings, business contacts, customers and contracts. Under normal circumstances, they would have needed some time to contact their accountant and legal counsel before embarking on such a major change in their lives.

Jesus continued on until he met the sons of Zebedee, James and John, two other brothers who were also working as commercial fishermen. It is possible that their mother was Salome, the sister of Mary, which, of course, would have made them first cousins of Jesus. The Lord made James and John the same offer He had just proposed to Peter and Andrew, with the same result. While they were preparing their nets to go out to work with their father, they *immediately* left the boat and followed Jesus (4:21–22).

READINESS

Jesus, as far as we know, had no formal training as a rabbi. Other men who volunteered to be his students may have boasted impressive resumes and credentials, but they were not chosen to be his disciples.

Many who were eager to follow him did not fully count the cost and could not commit to leaving behind their jobs, families, homes and friends. The prerequisite for joining Jesus' team was simply a desire to learn and obey despite the risks, and Jesus recognized such readiness in the hearts of the twelve.

Matthew Levi collected taxes for the Roman government—a reviled occupation because the tax law allowed extortion, bribery and violence as long as a certain quota was met. Matthew's call to be a disciple of Jesus came in a slightly different way than that of the Galilean fishermen. He met Jesus after the Lord had healed a demon-possessed boy and ruined the local pig farming industry. He had also incurred the wrath of the Pharisees and the teachers of the law for healing a paralyzed man and forgiving his sins (8:26–9:8).

As He continued on His way, Jesus passed Matthew busily employed in the trade that put a roof over his head, food on the table, and plenty of extra cash in his pocket, skimmed from those who could least afford it. Jesus simply said, "Follow me," and Matthew obeyed. Matthew didn't sleep on the decision overnight or ask for an employment contract that would guarantee his financial protection. He just got up and left with Jesus (9:9).

During the Roman occupation tax collectors in Israel were far down on the social ladder, just slightly above arsonists, murderers and armed robbers. Anyone hired by the Romans was seen as a collaborator of the worst sort, especially a tax collector. Tax collectors had to reach a certain level of assessment, and the Romans did not care where the money came from as long as it was handed over on time. Tax rates could be set arbitrarily and without interference from the government. For Matthew to walk away from such a lucrative position, there must have been a near miraculous intervention. There was, the moment he met Jesus Christ.

Matthew's own gospel records that Jesus had dinner with him, the disciples, other tax collectors and a group euphemistically lumped into the category of "sinners." While there Jesus was again confronted by the religious elite, the Pharisees, who demanded to know, "Why does your teacher eat with tax collectors and 'sinners'?"

MERCY, NOT SACRIFICE

Jesus said, "It is not the healthy who need a doctor, but the sick. But go and learn what this means: I desire mercy, not sacrifice. For I have not come to call the righteous, but sinners" (9:10–12). The Pharisees didn't get it. Jesus came to redeem and forgive sinners in need of restoring their relationship with God. They had a sin disease and only Jesus had the cure. For those who claimed to have no need or problem, Jesus could not and cannot help them.

Jesus went on to call other disciples as well. Matthew, a hated Roman collaborator, had to share the same campfire with Simon the Zealot. Matthew worked for the Romans and Simon loved to kill them.

Following one of his many miracles, Jesus was nearly overwhelmed by the press of people clamoring for healings and favors. He gave orders for His disciples to row across to the other side of the Sea of Galilee, where several more people volunteered to be His disciples. Normally one would be thrilled to have volunteer manpower ready to go and help, but in this case, the people were not responding to the Lord's direct leading.

One of the teachers of the law came to Him and said, "Teacher, I will follow you wherever you go." Jesus replied in one of His trademark nonanswers that offered an opportunity for self-discovery, "Foxes have holes and birds of the air have nests, but the Son of Man has no place to lay his head" (8:19–20). Following Him was not the path to security. Life would be fraught with difficulty because Jesus' followers would always be on the road with no place to call home.

Another person who volunteered to accompany Jesus asked to be excused long enough to bury his father. Jesus told him, "Follow me, and let the dead bury their own dead" (8:22). Perhaps this man wanted to wait until his aging father was gone before pursuing an adventure in ministry. But if we wait for the time to be right with all of the pieces of our lives safely in place, where is the faith? Where is the risk of stepping out into the unknown? Faith requires taking a dare, going into uncharted territory and relying on the Lord to see us through. Scripture defines faith as "being sure of what we hope for and certain of what we do not see" (Heb. 11:1). Hebrews goes on to say that "This is what the ancients were commended for" (11:2).

CALMING THE SEA

After Jesus had performed miracles and confirmed that He was not some wild-eyed, ranting prophet "wanna-be," he needed some space.

The crowds were clamoring for a healing, a favor or some other good deed. On the boat a terrific storm arose that threatened to sink the tiny vessel and everyone on board. The seas churned and the winds howled while Jesus slept during the disciple's first test of faith. Terrified, they went and woke Jesus, saying, "Lord, save us! We're going to drown!" (8:25).

Calmly and with full authority, Jesus replied, "You of little faith, why are you so afraid?" Jesus stood up and rebuked the winds and the waves as if scolding an unruly dog, and the sea was completely calm (8:26).

Amazed that even nature itself obeyed Jesus, for the first time the disciples may have realized that they had made a wise choice to follow such a man. It didn't take long for news of Jesus' exploits to spread throughout the land. He walked countless miles, reaching out to hurting people who needed to know the touch of a loving and forgiving God.

"These are the names of the twelve apostles: first, Simon (who is called Peter) and his brother Andrew; James son of Zebedee, and his brother John; Philip and Bartholomew (sometimes he is referred to as Nathaniel); Thomas and Matthew the tax collector; James son of Alphaeus, and Thaddaeus; Simon the Zealot and Judas Iscariot, who betrayed Him" (10:2–4). Surely Jesus could have recruited a better educated and more highly motivated group of guys. Yet he chose them because they were just like us: weak, fearful, ambitious, dishonest, quick to anger and slow to learn. The disciples typified the people Jesus referred to in the Beatitudes as being "poor in spirit."

Perhaps it is good that the Lord does not give us the entire picture when He calls us to do some form of ministry in His service. If He did, many of us would panic and run away before we ever got started. Had Jesus told Peter that he would walk on water, shame himself by denying that he knew Jesus, start a new Church and spread the news of redemption and grace to the Gentiles, he probably would have reconsidered the call. Had Jesus told Peter that he would be executed for his faith by being crucified upside down, Peter might have immediately rowed off into the sunset, never to be heard of again.

The same might be said for the rest of the disciples who left the security of their jobs and homes, all to follow Jesus. According to Christian tradition, Andrew was crucified on an X-shaped cross, James was beheaded, and others were stoned, shot with arrows or killed in equally heinous ways. John was persecuted and exiled to the isle of Patmos by the Roman emperor Diocletian. It was there that John received his greatest gift from the Lord, a vision of the end times as he recorded it in the Book of Revelation. Except for Judas, none of these ordinary men ever regretted throwing in their lot with Jesus Christ, because they were in for the adventure of a lifetime.

A Bird's Eye View
Zacchaeus

e⌀⌀⌀⌀

He was a squeezing, wrenching, grasping, scraping, clutching, covetous old sinner. No, not Ebenezer Scrooge from Charles Dickens' classic, *A Christmas Carol*, but the chief tax collector for the city of Jericho—Zacchaeus.

He was short. He was devious. He lied, cheated, stole, and threatened his way to financial gain while earning the undying enmity of everyone in town. Because he could swindle people with the protection and support of the Romans, who were eager to take their share of the spoil, he had few friends who wanted to share his wealth. Old Zach was about as crooked as a person could get after years of sin. Or, as my grandfather would say, "He had more twists than a corkscrew!"

While Jesus was passing through Jericho on one of His many trips across Israel, Zacchaeus decided he wanted to see the man who was causing such a stir (Luke 19:1–2). Yet he couldn't muscle his way through the crowd because he was short, and no one would defer to a "robber" who preyed on his fellow Jews. He became engulfed in the middle of the huge mob, unable to catch even a glimpse of Jesus.

SYCAMORE TREE

All Zach wanted to do was see Jesus and get a sense of what made Him such a celebrity. But if he were to talk to the Rabbi or even get close to him, some angry taxpayer might recognize him and seek revenge. So

Zacchaeus did the next best thing. Acting on a whim, he quickly scaled a sycamore fig tree to get a bird's eye view of Jesus' entry into town (19:4).

Although he tried to be inconspicuous, Jesus walked over to him and found him looking like a treed raccoon. Jesus looked up at him and said, "Zacchaeus, come down immediately. I must stay at your house today" (19:5). Jesus may have chuckled as he first glimpsed the short, perhaps rotund tax collector shinnying up the tree while trying to preserve some small measure of dignity.

Rather than make a fuss or try to hide, Zacchaeus came straight down . . . jumped down . . . fell down . . . and warmly welcomed Jesus. Not only did he welcome Jesus, but he also did something out of character. He invited Jesus home for dinner. Hosting a dinner cost money and Zach liked to keep his for himself.

That little dinner party must have made quite an impact on Zacchaeus, for he told Jesus and everyone camped out by his door like paparazzi waiting for a celebrity, "Look, Lord! Here and now I give half of my possessions to the poor, and if I have cheated anybody out of anything, I will pay back four times the amount" (19:8).

Not only did Jesus forgive him, but Zacchaeus made restitution—a necessary part of the redemption process. By refunding what he had stolen with quadrupled interest, he displayed the radical generosity of the Jubilee spirit that characterizes the kingdom of God.

When Jesus saw the depth of Zacchaeus's desire to change, He said, "Today salvation has come to this house, because this man, too, is a son of Abraham. For the Son of Man came to seek and to save what was lost" (19:9–10). Zacchaeus personified the true nature of repentance; he felt sorry enough for his sin to turn around and choose a different path for his life. Many people are sorry for sin—sorry they got caught, sorry they lost their families, sorry they ruined their marriage, sorry they wrecked their health, sorry they lost their reputation and self-respect, sorry they lost their possessions and positions, but not sorry they sinned and ruined their relationship with God.

Sometimes, even when you don't have all the advantages, the Lord can still break into your world and turn it right-side up again as He did for a short, tree-climbing sinner in need of a Savior.

Bizarre Biology!

Nicodemus

⁓⊙⊙⊙⁓

L earning is a wonderful thing. We do it all our lives, often without knowing it. Shortly after we were born, we bit down on our tiny hands to discover where we ended and the world began. We were busy learning the basic things of human existence. We soon learned that we were similar but distinct from the other people in our home—the ones called Mom and Dad and brothers and sisters.

We graduated to mastering body parts, colors, sounds, animal noises, letters, numbers, crossing the street, not talking to strangers and other useful information. Still, that was just the beginning of the learning process. The more we learn, we are reminded of how much more there is to grasp and master.

Remember though, that learning is different from education. Education is formal, specific and usually involves standardized tests, teachers, exams and report cards. Learning involves mistakes, false starts, pain, failure and success, usually without a diploma or a graduation ceremony. No one will cheer, no one will present you with a framed degree, no one will come to see you walk across a crowded stage to the strains of "Pomp and Circumstance." But if you keep your eyes open, your heart sensitive to the things of God and your mind free from preconceived ideas, the Lord will give you some fabulous "eureka" moments.

LAW AND TRADITION

One of those moments came for an old gentleman well-versed in the Law of Moses and the Hebrew faith—a renowned Pharisee named Nicodemus. The Pharisees had been self-appointed defenders of orthodox faith and practice ever since the Jews were freed from captivity following the exile.

The Pharisees followed the strict letter of the Law and tradition to ensure that the Hebrews would never again worship pagan idols, a practice that had plagued them ever since God led them out of slavery into the Promised Land. In their zeal to protect the faith, the Pharisees evolved into a legalistic sect and an intellectual elite that was set apart from the common people. There was almost no heart worship of God.

Jesus, in His preaching and teaching, never had anything good to say about the Pharisees, and he warned people not to imitate them. He referred to them as appearing healthy and vibrant on the outside, while inside where the heart and character mattered most, they were "whitewashed tombs filled with dead men's bones" (Matt. 23:27).

One night Jesus received a visit from Nicodemus, a respected Pharisee known for his wisdom and a member of the ruling council, the Sanhedrin. He might have spoken to Jesus somewhat patronizingly, "Rabbi, we know you are a teacher who has come from God. For no one could perform the miraculous signs you are doing if God were not with him" (John 3:1–2).

GLIMPSING THE KINGDOM

Nicodemus needed to ask his questions at night, far from the prying eyes and eavesdropping ears of the Pharisees, who might berate him for talking to this upstart preacher from Galilee. After all, Jesus claimed none of the academic credentials usually held by even the most neophyte Pharisee. Unlike the Pharisees, though, He spoke with power and authority and preached a provocative message that could not be found anywhere else. Compare hearing a lecture on the moon by a noted astronomer who has studied the topic for years with talking to Neil Armstrong, who actually set foot there in 1969.

Jesus sensed Nicodemus' genuine thirst for truth as he came seeking guidance on how to live a good life. Rather than give him easy answers, He dropped one of His usual non-answers, hoping to elicit more questions and bring about a revelation. Jesus declared, "I tell you the truth, no one can see the kingdom of God unless he is born again" (3:3).

We can almost feel Nicodemus' reaction of "Say what?" as he tried desperately to take in that shocking bit of bizarre biology.

"How can a man be born when he is old?" Nicodemus asked. "Surely he cannot enter a second time into his mother's womb to be born!" (3:4). *Impossible.* Nicodemus' head must have been spinning madly as he tried to imagine how an old man could possibly go back in time and revert to infancy.

Sensing his consternation, Jesus answered, "I tell you the truth, no one can enter the kingdom of God unless he is born of water and the Spirit. Flesh gives birth to flesh, but the Spirit gives birth to Spirit. You should not be surprised at my saying, 'You must be born again.' The wind blows wherever it pleases. You hear its sound, but you cannot tell where it comes from or where it is going. So it is with everyone born of the Spirit" (3:3–8).

"How can this be?" Nicodemus asked (3:9). He must have thought to himself, *I ask a simple question and He gives me water and spirit, blowing wind and spirit birth. I get the part of flesh giving birth to flesh and wind blowing where it chooses upon whomever it chooses. I can understand that much. God reveals Himself to those He chooses when they are ready to accept and understand what is coming. I hate to tell you, though, Jesus, I still don't get it.*

Jesus reminded Nicodemus that as one of Israel's foremost teachers, he should be well-versed in theological understanding, not merely the observance of rules and liturgy that had little to do with spiritual life (3:10). Jesus said, "I tell you the truth, we speak of what we know, and we testify to what we have seen, but still you people do not accept our testimony. I have spoken to you of earthly things and you do not believe; how then will you believe if I speak of heavenly things? No one has ever gone into heaven except the one who came from heaven—the Son of Man" (3:11–13).

Rather than explain the Law, Jesus challenged Nicodemus to take a hard look at his beliefs about the things of God. Jesus said that He told the truth as the embodiment of the things of heaven. But if people cannot grasp what is earthly and obvious, how can they fully appreciate heavenly things that can only be ascertained by someone who has knowledge of them?

PERFECT SACRIFICE

This exchange between Master and seeker takes place early in the book of John. Yet even then Jesus hinted that His ministry would be revolutionary and transformational, because it would be based not on education but on His perfect sacrifice. Jesus cited a precedent that all good Hebrew teachers would remember, that of Moses and the brass serpent in the book of Exodus. When the people in the wilderness were bitten by poisonous snakes as punishment from God, they had only to look in faith at the brass snake and they would recover—no examinations, no doctors, no logical explanation of the snake's curative powers—just faith and obedience. In a similar way, Jesus said that He "must be lifted up" not for public acclaim, but put to death high on a Roman cross so that everyone who believes in Christ might have eternal life.

Nicodemus' quest for the truth about Jesus' mission and plan led to the passage in the Bible that has brought grace and peace to millions over the centuries and around the world: "For God so loved the world that He gave His one and only Son, that whoever believes in Him shall not perish but have eternal life. For God did not send his Son into the world to condemn the world, but to save the world through Him. Whoever believes in Him is not condemned, but whoever does not believe stands condemned already because he has not believed in the name of God's one and only Son" (3:16–18).

Those verses contain the core of Christian theology. They evoke a hope that is twofold—for restoration of a divine relationship marred by failure, disobedience, and suffering, and for a life beyond our limited and flawed human existence.

While Jesus drew harsh criticism for challenging the status quo, many people still heard Him and accepted His message, believing Him to be the Son of God. Even the common folk realized that while Jesus taught and preached openly, the Pharisees just grumbled among themselves. They grumbled but could do nothing to confront the One they branded as a heretic for breaching orthodox faith and practice. "Here he is, speaking publicly, and they are not saying a word to him. Have the authorities really concluded that he is the Christ?" (7:26).

SILENCING JESUS

In order to silence Jesus, the Pharisees plotted to send the temple guards to arrest Him. But the people were divided; some accepted Jesus while others believed Him to be a threat and a fraud. "Finally the temple guards went back to the chief priests and Pharisees, who asked them, "Why didn't you bring Him in?" "No one ever spoke the way this man does," the guards declared (7:44–46). That was exactly what the Pharisees did not want to hear.

Seeing that the Pharisees were planning to kill Jesus to silence him, Nicodemus was the first person to raise a common sense argument. "Does our law condemn anyone without first hearing him to find out what he is doing?" (7:50). Even in those days an accused person had some right of due process, as limited as that might be under the Roman occupation.

By this time, though, the Pharisees, determined to protect their own power and prestige by whatever means necessary, had no intention of allowing Jesus to teach and preach openly. Nicodemus could only diffuse the situation temporarily, for it would be just a matter of time before the Pharisees turned to violence. The death of one prophet, more or less, seemed a small price to pay to maintain the status quo, and even someone like Nicodemus could do nothing to stop it. All Nicodemus could do was to comfort and aid Jesus' grieving family after the Pharisees got their way, ending with Jesus' execution on Golgotha.

After the grisly work was done, Joseph of Arimathea, a disciple and follower of Jesus, went to Pilate and begged to take Jesus' body so that He could be given a proper burial. Joseph, quite vocal in dealing with Pilate after Jesus was dead, was a secret disciple since he feared the Pharisees and the ruling Jewish council (19:38). He and Nicodemus assisted in removing Jesus' body to a place of burial where it could be safe. There they wrapped Jesus' body in linen with burial spices and laid Him in a tomb before sundown and the celebration of Passover. Joseph had

Jesus buried in a tomb that had been carved out of rock in preparation for Joseph's own death (19:39–42).

Once Nicodemus heard the news of Jesus' resurrection, did that late-night conversation about birth and rebirth, life, death and life eternal begin to make more sense?

Never Running Dry

The Woman at the Well

⤷⊙⊚⊙↩

We all have a past filled with things we have done very well, some less well and some we would just as soon forget. Sometimes our old choices return to haunt us and cloud our thoughts, making it almost impossible to dream of something better. Although Scripture reminds us that "all have sinned and fallen short of the glory of God," it does not leave us to wallow in despair without hope and the possibility of redemption. We pray for the grace to truly believe we are forgiven, break free of guilt, leave the past behind, and make more godly choices in the future.

In studying Scripture we soon appreciate the way that Jesus taught. He never gave away the answer to a question until the seeker had an opportunity to discover what was hidden in plain sight. He allowed ample time for profound discomfort before applying the healing comfort of forgiveness, with no thought to social or cultural convention. Political correctness was never high on Jesus' agenda, for He rarely cared about others' opinions as long as He was doing His Father's will. Such was the case as He traveled from Galilee down to Judea, passing right through the heart of Samaria.

Good Jews never passed through Samaria unless it was absolutely necessary. They would rather cross to the other side of the Jordan River than pass through Samaria. It would be like going from Syracuse, New York to Baltimore, Maryland via New Jersey and Delaware just to avoid Pennsylvania—not the recommended AAA route to be sure.

OUTCASTS

Jews had shunned the Samaritans as heretics ever since the days of captivity and exile as recorded in the Old Testament. After deporting all those with social and economic status, the conquering Assyrians brought in foreigners who intermarried with the Jews still living in that part of Israel. Samaritans had just enough Jewish theology to make them relatives without the purity of a traceable family line to make them brothers. The city of Samaria was the capital and center of worship, while Jerusalem was the capital and worship center of Israel.

Jesus, in typical defiance of social tradition, had decided to go through Samaria instead of around it, and he was resting from His long walk in the town of Sychar. Sychar was located near the plot of land that Jacob had given to Joseph as part of his inheritance. It had a decent well that could serve the needs of the town and the surrounding area (John 4:4–6). Jesus arrived at the well in the center of town around noon, the hottest part of the day. By then most women would have come and gone hours ago, before it became too hot to move about without risking heat stroke. The disciples, meanwhile, had gone to buy food for lunch (4:8).

When the Samaritan woman arrived to draw water, Jesus said to her, "Will you give me a drink?" (4:7). Jesus had just asked a hated Samaritan, and a woman at that, for a drink. In their day and time, such an exchange simply didn't take place in polite society. John records the woman's straightforward reply to the request. Knowing that Jews and Samaritans despised each other, much like modern day Israelis and Arabs, she said, "You are a Jew and I am a Samaritan woman. How can you ask me for a drink?" (4:9).

BRIDGING THE GAP

Jesus could have said, "There isn't anyone here and I can't find the bucket," or "I have a bad back." Instead, He turned the response around in order to teach her about the grace of redemption. Clearly she must have been a social pariah, because she had timed her arrival at the well to avoid encountering anybody else. Undoubtedly she sought to avoid the cutting comments and brutal stares of the women who disapproved of her. Jesus answered, "If you knew the gift of God and who it is that asks you for a drink, you would have asked Him and He would have given you living water" (4:10).

She must have been puzzled by his statement—living water from a man who has no canteen, rope or other means to retrieve the water? She tried to be as understanding as possible, enjoying a rare bit of conversation with another human being.

"Sir," the woman said, "you have nothing to draw with and the well is deep. Where can you get this living water? Are you greater than our father Jacob, who gave us the well and drank from it himself, as did also his sons and his flocks and herds?" (4:11–12). She knew that the history of the well was intertwined with both Jews and Samaritans. But she was still stuck on the well and the need to draw water daily in a hostile environment. Perhaps she thought to herself, *Does this man mean living water like in the stories of Moses and the manna in the wilderness? Does He have a way to get water so that I won't have to listen to a bunch of busybodies again?*

Jesus returned to the main point of the conversation. It wasn't about water—it was about a relationship with God—one that is deep, lasting and satisfying in this life and throughout eternity. Jesus answered, "Everyone who drinks this water will be thirsty again, but whoever drinks the water I give him will never thirst. Indeed, the water I give him will become in him a spring of water welling up to eternal life" (4:13–14).

"Sir," the woman replied, "give me this water so that I won't get thirsty and have to keep coming here to draw water" (4:15). She was making progress but she still didn't get it. She was still locked into the earthly necessity of obtaining H2O—not living in a personal relationship with God. The Samaritans worshipped the same God as the Jews but in a different place and in ways that were not acceptable to each other. The Samaritans' religion consisted of a blend of traditional Judaism, idol worship and the practice of magic.

Rather than pursue a theological debate or even explain the importance of salvation as a lifelong journey, Jesus threw her a curve to let her know he was talking about more than just an academic exercise on water.

He told her, "Go, call your husband and come back" (4:16).

NO ORDINARY TRAVELER

Apparently without skipping a beat, the Samaritan woman replied that she had no husband. Jesus agreed with her, "You are right when you say you have no husband. The fact is, you have had five husbands, and the man you now have is not your husband. What you have just said is quite true" (4:17–18).

The woman did not try to explain the reasons for her many failed relationships. Under Jewish law a man could file for divorce for any number of trivial reasons, but a wife could not divorce her husband without his consent. In first century Israel, women were viewed as little better than slaves on the social ladder. They had no rights, rarely owned property, and remained largely confined to their homes. Midwifery was perhaps the only honorable public occupation in which a woman could be employed. Because of such gross gender inequalities, divorced women, as well as widows, frequently fought an uphill battle for economic survival. Prostitution was not an uncommon response to the problem.

The woman knew that Jesus was no ordinary traveler. "Sir," the woman said respectfully, "I can see that you are a prophet." She went on to tell of her faith. "Our fathers worshipped on this mountain, but you Jews claim that the place where we must worship is in Jerusalem" (4:20).

The Lord then offered her insight into the true nature of worship, apart from place, tradition, history or ethnicity. Jesus declared, "Believe me, woman, a time is coming when you will worship the Father neither on this mountain nor in Jerusalem. You Samaritans worship what you do not know; we worship what we do know, for salvation is from the Jews. Yet a time is coming and has now come when the true worshippers will worship the Father in spirit and truth, for they are the kind of worshippers the Father seeks. God is spirit, and His worshippers must worship in spirit and in truth" (4:21–24). His reference to "you Samaritans" was not intended to be judgmental but to state what they both believed—that the Messiah, according to prophecy, would come to the Jews first. Jesus in no way treated the Samaritan woman like a second-class class citizen who was unworthy of the Lord's blessings.

The woman said, "I know that Messiah" (called Christ) "is coming. When He comes, he will explain everything to us" (4:25). In other words, *I know what the Scripture says. Someday all this will be sorted out so it makes sense even to people like me.*

Then Jesus declared to her perhaps the greatest news of all time, "I who speak to you am He" (4:26).

There are many "Aha" moments in Scripture—Moses falling prostrate before the burning bush, Noah receiving God's orders to build the Ark, Abraham's ecstasy when Isaac's life was spared, and the Lord speaking directly to Moses and many other prophets. Surely this story is in the same company. An anonymous woman, spurned and alone, probably not a "respectable" member of a local congregation, heard the declaration of the Messiah.

Jesus rarely came out and confirmed that he was the Messiah, choosing instead to let His miracles speak for Him. His supernatural acts were intended to show people that His power emanated from the Father who sent Him. He usually asked, "Who do you say that I am?" to allow for personal discovery rather than direct revelation. He could sense the woman's longing for something more—a healing of the emotions that went deeper than curing leprosy, paralysis or even death. Although diseases can kill the body, emotional suffering can destroy both the body and the spirit.

ETERNAL LIVING

As the visit drew to a close, the disciples returned from their errands and lunch. They were surprised to see Jesus talking to the woman, because conversation between the sexes was a clear breach of social custom. The look on Jesus' face and the tone of His voice must have signaled that He was involved in the deep things of God. The woman left her water jar, a fairly expensive and essential piece of equipment, and ran to tell anyone in town who would listen what had just happened and who she had just met. She acknowledged her sins before God and the people and invited them all to "Come, see a man who told me everything I ever did. Could this be the Christ?"(4:29). All at once she became one of the first evangelists to spread the news of the gospel.

Not content with a drink of water and some pleasant theological conversation, and willing to endure the pain of a life-changing encounter, she was never the same again. What a wonderful decision she made to get Jesus a drink of water. And we don't even know her name. Jesus knows and that is all that matters. She did not have all the information about her relationship with Him, but she was still marvelously transformed, encouraged and healed.

The All-Star Pharisee

Paul

⋙⊙⊙⋘

As I have studied the Bible, I often wonder if Paul, formerly known as Saul, was named for the first king of Israel. If so, perhaps the Lord changed his name (Acts 13:9) so His greatest writer, teacher, evangelist and church planter would not be confused with Israel's first and failed king.

Paul was not the only one to have his name changed by the Lord—Abram became Abraham, Jacob became Israel and Simon became Peter. All of these name changes symbolized greater trust and opportunity for ministry.

In the case of Paul, perhaps no one wanted to be reminded of an ineffective and ungodly monarch who led Israel down the path of civil war. The Bible slips in Saul's name change almost as an aside: "Paul who was also called Saul, filled with the Holy Spirit . . ." The catalyst for the name change and new ministry must have come from being infused with the Holy Spirit.

CREDENTIALS

Paul had an advantage over Jesus' other disciples. Rather than being a fisherman, tax collector or zealot—occupations not requiring an impressive resume—Paul was a Pharisee, and one of the best. As one of the hyper-spiritual "separated ones," he prided himself on scrupulously keeping both the rules of Mosaic Law as well as all of its minute interpretations and applications. If there were prizes for Pharasaic excellence, Paul would have won the Nobel, the Pulitzer and the Heisman. He was an all-star legalistic rule keeper if ever there was one.

Paul summarizes his spiritual resume in Philippians 3:4–6. "If anyone else thinks he has reasons to put confidence in the flesh, I have more: circumcised on the eighth day, of the people of Israel, of the tribe of Benjamin, a Hebrew of Hebrews; in regard to the law, a Pharisee; as for zeal, persecuting the church; as for legalistic righteousness, faultless."

Most of the time, such credentials would more than suffice except that Paul, after a personal encounter with the Risen Savior, considered all of them to be worthless. He goes on to say,

> *But whatever was to my profit I now consider loss for the sake of Christ. What is more, I consider everything a loss compared to the surpassing greatness of knowing Christ Jesus my Lord, for whose sake I have lost all things. I consider them rubbish, that I may gain Christ and be found in Him, not having a righteousness of my own that comes from the law, but that which is through faith in Christ—the righteousness that comes from God and is by faith. I want to know Christ and the power of His resurrection and the fellowship of sharing in His sufferings, becoming like Him in his death, and so, somehow, to attain to the resurrection from the dead. Not that I have already obtained all this, or have already been made perfect, but I press on to take hold of that for which Christ Jesus took hold of me. Brothers, I do not consider myself yet to have taken hold of it. But one thing I do: Forgetting what is behind and straining toward what is ahead, I press on toward the goal to win the prize for which God has called me heavenward in Christ Jesus* (Philippians 3:7–14).

Paul ended his ministry with these words penned in a cell in Rome, where Christian tradition says he awaited execution for his faith.

STEPHEN

We first find Paul (then Saul) on the scene at the stoning of Stephen, Christianity's first martyr (Acts 6–7). As recorded in Acts 6: 1–7, Stephen and several others had been chosen to help deliver food to the elderly and widows in Jerusalem, which freed up the apostles to preach, teach and grow the Church. Those who had lived and worked side by side with Jesus could spread the gospel first hand through an effective division of labor and responsibility.

It didn't take long for the Pharisees, self-appointed keepers of orthodoxy, to resent the popularity and joyful ministry of Jesus' followers. Scripture says that Stephen, "a man full of God's grace and power, did great wonders and miracles among the people. Opposition arose . . . These men began to argue with Stephen, but they could not stand up against his wisdom or by the Spirit by which he spoke" (6:8–10).

In those days, if all else failed, people could accuse an opponent of blasphemy, find witnesses willing to commit perjury and then condemn the person publicly. Stephen, condemned and convicted without proof or credible testimony, was stoned to death. Before he died he eloquently described the foundation and fruition of Christianity, explaining how his accusers had tried to thwart the plans of God. He declared that rather than being keepers of orthodox theology, detractors of the new faith were actually frustrating God's will.

And Saul was there "giving approval to his death. On that day a great persecution broke out against the church at Jerusalem, and all except the apostles were scattered throughout Judea and Samaria" (8:1). Following Stephen's execution, persecution erupted against the Church, and everyone except the apostles either fled or went into hiding. Had this happened before Pentecost, the apostles either would have been the first to run or been found cowering under their beds. Now, filled with and empowered by the Holy Spirit, they were a fearless force.

Saul started a personal crusade of religious cleansing and eradication, going from house to house ferreting out Christians as they prayed and met together, and hauling them off to prison. After being tortured and imprisoned, they could either recant their faith or face execution (8:3–4).

PERSECUTION

Little did Saul know that the more he persecuted Jesus' followers and drove them out of Jerusalem, the further the influence of the gospel would spread. And the more he opposed them, the more he succeeded in strengthening, not weakening, their faith. Ironically, this scattering of believers began to fulfill Jesus' promise that the apostles would be His witnesses "in Jerusalem, and in all Judea and Samaria, and to the ends of the earth" (1:8). Saul obtained warrants from the High Priest to arrest Christians in Damascus (modern day Syria) and drag them to Jerusalem (9:1–2). All was going according to plan, but the Lord has a unique way of taking our agenda and turning it upside down to carry out his will.

As Saul walked along the road, he was struck by a light from heaven that brought him to his knees in the middle of the dusty road. Falling to the ground, he heard a voice cry out to him, "Saul, Saul, why do you persecute me?"

He asked, "Who are you, Lord?"

Maybe Saul expected an angel or even the voice of the Almighty. Instead he heard, "I am Jesus, whom you are persecuting" (9:3–5). The blinding light that struck Saul could have been the radiance of the *Shekinah*, the glory of God that had not been seen for many generations. Jesus replied with the phrase reserved for God alone, I AM—the same name God used when Moses asked "who shall I say sent me" to let the Hebrews go from Egypt. I AM—past, present, future, without need, without equal, all-powerful and self-sustaining. It was a name Saul would have known quite well, although good Pharisees did not speak the name of God out of reverence for His majesty and awe.

Saul fell with his face to the ground, keeping quiet and waiting for instructions.

Jesus said, "Now get up and go into the city, and you will be told what you must do" (9:6).

Saul collected his wits and stood up, feeling relatively safe in that he was still alive. When he got to his feet, he discovered that he was blind, no doubt from the radiant glory of the Lord. Looking on the face of Jesus would be like staring directly at the noonday sun without any protection. Saul's servants led him into Damascus where he stayed at the home of Judas on Straight Street. Scripture indicates that for three days, he fasted and no doubt prayed intently about his future since the Lord now had his undivided attention. (9:8–9).

ANANIAS

The Lord then spoke to a disciple named Ananias in a vision. "Go to the house of Judas on Straight Street and ask for a man from Tarsus named Saul, for he is praying. In a vision he has seen a man named Ananias come and place his hands on him to restore his sight" (9:10–12).

Ananias knew about the persecution in and around Jerusalem and proceeded to remind the Lord of Saul's intentions. Perhaps he hoped the Lord would reconsider this incredible plan.

The Lord said to Ananias, "Go! This man is my chosen instrument to carry my name before the Gentiles and their kings and before the people of Israel. I will show him how much he must suffer for my name" (9:15–16). Ananias was told simply to obey and not to worry about the outcome. The Lord was not going to do Saul any favors, though. He would commission, equip and empower him, and make him a wonderful blessing for Jews and Gentiles alike, but he would suffer too, much like the simple folk he had been persecuting.

Putting aside his fear and personal mistrust, Ananias went to Judas' house as commanded. Placing his hands on Saul, he said, "Brother Saul, the Lord—Jesus, who appeared to you on the road as you were coming here—has sent me so that you may see again and be filled with the Holy Spirit" (19:17).

With no snappy comebacks, rationalizations, or quoting of his theological resume, Saul sat before Ananias quietly and gratefully. Scripture says that as soon as Ananias prayed, "something like scales fell from Saul's eyes, and he could see again. He got up and was baptized" (19:18). After eating some food and regaining his strength, he spent time with believers in Damascus to learn about their newfound faith in Christ. He went to the local synagogues and preached that Jesus was the Son of God. Some people must have been skeptical, others amazed and perplexed by his sudden and radical transformation. Yet despite their questions and real concerns for their safety, Saul kept on preaching about Jesus and "baffled the Jews living in Damascus by proving that Jesus is the Christ" (9:22).

A BOLD PREACHER

Saul spent three years alone in the Arabian Desert to prepare for his new ministry. Once he became known as Paul (his name indicated his status as a Roman citizen), he gradually won the trust of other believers as well as new converts to the Jesus movement. He also managed to alienate some of his radically orthodox Jewish brothers from Jerusalem and Greece, who were conspiring to kill him.

As a bold preacher of the gospel, Paul would be on the receiving end of the same persecution that he had engaged in so vehemently. His conversion spurred an unparalleled witness to Christianity and to readers of the Bible that he would later help to write. None of that would have happened if Paul had played it safe and ignored the direct command of the Lord that day on the road to Damascus.

Paul could have chosen to ignore Jesus' command to seek out Ananias and remained content to stay a blind victim. He could have blamed the Lord for his blindness, waived his own accountability and expectations, and stayed on the sidelines. Instead, he took a chance and carried out God's plan all the way from Damascus to Rome, where scholars say he was finally executed for the sake of the gospel he had once tried to eradicate. Good thing he made the right decision, or today we might be missing most of the New Testament and priceless knowledge about how to grow in faith with Jesus Christ.

Draw the Circle Wide

Philip and the Ethiopian

⋘⊚⊙⊚⋙

The book of Acts relates the remarkable story of Philip and the eunuch from Ethiopia, who was among the first Gentile converts to Christianity. Philip had been actively witnessing in Samaria, where an ethnically mixed group of people espoused a theology integrating Judaism with idol worship. The issues of bloodline, a separate Temple and faith differences had driven great enmity between Jews and Samaritans over the centuries. Jesus, of course, had already preached the gospel in Samaria, and after his resurrection, the Spirit led Philip, Peter and John there to perform miraculous signs and healings. The disciples were only beginning to understand the depth and breath of a gospel that knows no limits.

An angel of the Lord sent Philip to the desert road "that goes down from Jerusalem to Gaza," a remote location in the wilderness of Judea (Acts 8:26). Along the way he met an exotic Ethiopian—a eunuch in charge of the treasury of Queen Candace, who had been in Jerusalem to worship (8:27). As Philip walked past the official's chariot, he found this influential African official engrossed in reading the book of Isaiah. The Spirit told Philip, "Go to that chariot and stay near it" (8:29), giving him an extraordinary chance to proclaim the infinite circle of God's grace.

Approaching the chariot, he heard the Ethiopian reading the Hebrew scroll out loud and asked him, "Do you understand what you are reading?" (8:30).

INTERPRETING THE WORD

"How can I," he asked, "unless someone explains it to me?" Inviting
Philip to join him in the royal carriage (8:31), he read aloud the text that
spoke of the suffering savior. "He was led like a sheep to the slaughter,
and as a lamb before the shearer is silent, so He did not open his mouth.
In His humiliation he was deprived of justice. Who can speak of His descendants? For His life was taken from the earth" (8:32–33). The
Ethiopian inquired whether this passage referred to the prophet Isaiah
or to someone else.

Presented with an opening he could drive a truck through, Philip
seized the moment to tell the man the story of Jesus of Nazareth—His
birth, mission, life, death, resurrection and coming reign, until he truly
believed that Jesus was indeed the Messiah. Knowing the traditions of
the Jews and John the Baptist, the Ethiopian took the next step of faith
and asked to be baptized. After stopping the chariot, he found an oasis
in the desert (no small coincidence) where Philip baptized him as a sign
of new life in Christ.

For the Ethiopian, salvation transcended race, nationality, ethnicity,
and his physical condition as a eunuch. Because of that condition, under Jewish law he would have been a social outcast and excluded from
the worship community of Israel (Deut. 23:1). Surely he would have
been barred from the Temple in Jerusalem, where he had recently ac-
companied the Queen.

Later on Paul emphasized the radical inclusivity of the gospel in one
of the most famous passages in the New Testament: "You are all sons of
God through faith in Christ Jesus, for all of you who were baptized into
Christ have clothed yourselves with Christ. There is nether Jew nor
Greek, slave nor free, male nor female, for you are all one in Christ Je-
sus" (Gal. 3:26–28).

As the two men emerged from the water dripping wet and filled with
an inexpressible joy, "the Spirit of the Lord suddenly took Philip away,
and the eunuch did not see him again, but went on his way rejoicing"
(8:39).

Philip was one of the Lord's first evangelists, and the Ethiopian was
among the first gentiles outside of Israel to accept the gospel. Because
of his openness and a teachable spirit the eunuch sought Scriptural understanding from Philip, and then he chose to act upon what he had

learned. This poignant story illustrates the availability of the Christian message to all who would hear and believe it. It inspires believers to seize every opportunity within reach to draw the circle wide in the name of Jesus Christ.

"C'mon Over to My House And Start a Church"
Lydia

eↄ੭◎ਕ

Throughout Paul's three missionary journeys and his final trip to plead his case for Christ before the emperor in Rome, he may have slept in more places than George Washington. He depended on the hospitality of others who graciously opened their homes to him.

During the last days of his life, he was chained between two guards. Surely he preached to them whether they were asleep or not. Most likely, they tried to look as if they were sleeping, but Paul would have continued talking and witnessing as though they were wide awake.

Paul occasionally received visions from God. On one of those nights, he had a vision of a man from Macedonia (a Roman province in Greece) who was pleading with him to "Come over and help us" (Acts 16:9). That was all the urging Paul needed to make plans to go to Macedonia and preach the gospel in that part of Europe (19:10).

Paul and his companions sailed from Troas and headed straight for Samothrace. After a brief overnight layover, they sailed on to Neapolis and then to the Roman colony of Philippi—a center of worship and trade and the leading city in Macedonia (16:11–12).

PREACHER AND SALESMAN

Paul was nothing if not an expert preacher and salesman for Jesus, and he usually knew where he could find an audience. He always headed first to the local synagogue, where he could be sure to meet men who were well-versed in Judaism. And besides that, what small town Hebrew congregation would balk at all having the world's premier Pharisee and expert in the Law visit and teach their congregation?

Leaving the synagogue to seek another place of prayer, Paul walked down to the river where the local women met to wash clothes—perhaps a Philippian version of the local laundromat. Even though he was in Gentile country, this action signaled a powerful testimony to his transformation since his days as a Pharisee. As a Pharisee he would never have done anything on the Sabbath that remotely resembled work, and just as certainly, he would not have chosen women as his target audience. That would have been the old Paul, not the new, transformed, Spirit-filled Paul. He witnessed and taught the women, not in a grand stadium crusade, but during the course of their daily responsibilities. Isn't that just like God though, to meet us in the daily routine of life, and do something surprising?

TRUE BELIEVER

"One of those listening was a woman named Lydia, a dealer in purple cloth from the city of Thyatira, who was a worshipper of God. The Lord opened her heart to respond to Paul's message" (16:14). Thyatira must have been a perilous location to worship God because in Revelation 3, we read that it was the place of Satan's throne. Since Lydia dealt in purple cloth—a material used by royalty since the dye was rare and expensive—we know that she had talents for business as well as gifts for ministry.

Lydia heard the gospel, accepted the message of grace and forgiveness, and decided to be baptized as a disciple of Jesus Christ. In a single verse of Scripture she went from finding salvation as a life to a baptism with her entire family. After joining the fledgling church in Philippi, Lydia invited Paul to her home, not only for hospitality's sake but to use as his church-planting center of operations (16:15).

Lydia witnessed to her whole family by being teachable, sociable, hospitable and generous. Without her decision and her willingness to help Paul, the ministry and outreach in Philippi might have been frustrated and ended up a failure, as it did in Lystra, just down the road.

The Lord enacts miracles, sometimes spectacular ones, where the lame walk, the blind see and the dead are raised to life. But in this case, God performed the miraculous in the mundane—by changing the heart of one generous lady. Paul may have been the star of the story, but without Lydia, he might have been living out on the streets of Philippi.

Free to Be

The Jailer in Philippi

⋐ⓈⒼⓈ⋑

Paul's ministry in Philippi was off and running in fine form. Lydia's home provided a place to live, worship and teach, and possibly even a small workshop where he could make tents and earn a few *drachma* to buy groceries. You would think that his work in Philippi would flourish and go from victory to victory in an ever-increasing atmosphere of revival and soul-winning glory. But that is not what happened. As the spin on the old adage goes, "It is always darkest—just before it goes completely black!"

Paul wasn't trying to be confrontational. All he wanted was to find a good place to pray and to go about his business of soul-winning. However, as is often the case whenever we begin to get close to the Lord and His work for us, his life became complex and uncomfortable.

FORTUNE TELLER

Paul and his companions, on their way to a prayer meeting, met a slave girl who was able to predict the future—for a price. Scripture says that she "earned a great deal of money for her owners by fortune telling" (Acts 16:16). Apparently she had a spirit of divination that gave her the power to see the future.

For many days the girl, possessed by the spirits that controlled her, shadowed Paul and his companions, shouting, "These men are servants of the Most High God, who are telling you the way to be saved" (16:17).

She delivered her message not to encourage, but to deride, devalue and denigrate Paul and the Lord he served.

Paul, growing weary of the slave girl's demented harangue, turned to her and ordered the spirit of divination to leave her body (16:18). And it did, completely and quietly, like a misbehaving dog firmly disciplined by its master. But as the spirit departed, so did her supposed psychic abilities—and any potential earnings for her employers. Ministry to women doing laundry by the river was one thing, but interfering with the income of some dangerous and powerful men was another. Paul was in big trouble.

The slave girl's owners seized Paul and Silas, his traveling partner, and dragged them to the marketplace to face the authorities. Then the authorities brought them before the magistrates, saying, "These men are Jews, and are throwing our city into an uproar by advocating customs unlawful for us Romans to accept or practice" (16:19–20). They made sure to note that Paul and Silas were Jews, foreigners and strangers while they were local taxpayers and law-abiding citizens.

Now that the situation had morphed into a major spectacle, the local crowd joined the fray and further heightened the drama. Since the slave girl's owners were important and influential, there was no way the magistrates could release Paul and Silas with merely a warning or a light fine (16:22).

The magistrates ordered Paul and Silas to be arrested, beaten and incarcerated—all to please the mob and to guarantee future contributions to their campaign war chests. Paul and Silas were stripped, beaten and tossed into prison with strict orders to the jailer to guard them carefully (16:22–23). The jailer locked them in a secure inside cell and put their feet in stocks so there would be no chance for escape (16:24).

EARTHQUAKE

Rather than create a disturbance by loudly protesting their innocence, Paul and Silas prayed and sang hymns while the other prisoners listened. Suddenly, around midnight, there was such a violent earthquake that the jail was rocked on its foundation, and everyone's chains came loose.

The jailer awoke to the racket and saw all the cell doors spring open. He pulled out his sword and instead of defending the jail from would be escapees, prepared to take his own life. He knew the regulations—lose a prisoner, lose your life (16:25–27).

Before the jailer could hurt himself, Paul shouted, "Don't harm yourself! We are all here!" (16:28). The jailer must have expected everyone to flee as fast as possible or to try and ambush the guards on duty. When he called for lighting, he was amazed that all of the prisoners were accounted for with no riot or mass exodus. Realizing that Paul and Silas somehow stood at the center of his miracle, the jailer rushed in and fell trembling at their feet. Trembling with fear, trembling with awe, trembling with excitement.

The jailer showed no interest in a rational explanation for the events that had just transpired. He simply asked, "Sirs, what must I do to be saved?" (16:30). He knew that Paul and Silas were men of God, and he wanted to be forgiven and to begin a new life with the Lord. Suddenly, his job didn't count for much in light of what he had just witnessed.

Paul replied, "Believe in the Lord Jesus, and you will be saved—you and your household" (16:31). He did not mean that one man's confession and acceptance would save others, since that is a choice we need to make individually. The key is belief and trust, and there is no such thing as grace by proxy. Paul simply meant that an invitation to salvation would carry more weight with the jailer's household once his family had seen first-hand the dramatic change in him.

Paul and Silas went on to explain many more spiritual concepts to the jailer and his family. The jailer took Paul and Silas aside and tended to their wounds. And before the night was over, not only was the jail secured again, but the jailer and all his family were baptized inside the prison.

Scripture says that "the jailer brought them into his house and set a meal before them; he was filled with joy because he had come to believe in God—he and his whole family" (16:34). What an evening that must have been with the whole group of them crying, laughing, praying and singing.

CITIZENSHIP

The next morning, perhaps after cleaning up from the late-night earthquake, the magistrates sent officials to the jail to release Paul and Silas. The jailer entered and passed along the news. "The magistrates have ordered that you and Silas be released. Now you can leave. Go in peace" (16:36).

They would not leave, though, without first having their say. Paul told the officers: "They [the magistrates, the officials and the mob] beat us publicly without a trial, even though we are Roman citizens, and threw us into prison. And now do they want to get rid of us quietly? No! Let them come themselves and escort us out" (16:36).

When the officers "reported this to the magistrates, and when they heard that Paul and Silas were Roman citizens, they were alarmed" (16:38). Citizenship with all its benefits and perks was reserved for people of great power, wealth and influence. The magistrates realized that they had just beaten and locked up two prominent people with ties to the Roman government without charge or due process. They could have been subjected to similar treatment if Paul had chosen to exercise his rights as a Roman citizen.

The magistrates arrived to placate Paul and Silas and "escorted them from the prison, requesting them to leave the city" (16:39). They made their request—not an order—gently, with humble apology and considerable terror about their own fates.

After leaving the prison, Paul and Silas "went to Lydia's house, where they met with the brothers and encouraged them. Then they left" (16:40). They returned to the home of the same Lydia who had just joined the family of God. There must have been quite a celebration before the two evangelists hit the road again.

The most important question we can ever ask, "What must I do to be saved?" We sometimes have difficulty trying to explain the theology of Christian salvation, when it is really quite simple—"Believe in the Lord Jesus, and you will be saved." The single best choice you could ever make.

More Than He Bargained For

The Prodigal Son

cᲖᎧᏮᎧᏫ

The parable of the Prodigal Son is a popular gospel story with a palpable lesson on grace, forgiveness, obedience and reconciliation. Although the son is the primary figure, the parable might as well be called The Parable of the Loving Father. Both characters are essential for the story to make sense and for us to gain a deeper understanding of the nature of God. A parable is often described as "an earthy story with a heavenly meaning," or an everyday situation that contains a universal application. Jesus frequently taught with parables so that His listeners could find themselves in the story and discover their need for grace and growth.

We can all find ourselves in this story, especially if we have children or have ever made a bad decision and wished for another chance to make things right. By shifting the focus from the son to the father who welcomed him home, we can move toward a clearer image of God. Jesus taught this parable to show that God's love is unconditional, eternal and far in excess of anything we deserve. The Lord offers grace when we deserve punishment; He offers mercy when we deserve justice. This parable resonates with every child eager to assert independence, and every parent of a headstrong or rebellious child. It is loved because it ends well, with restoration, recovered affection and coming home—the favorite destination of travelers everywhere.

MANY LAYERS

There are enough layers of meaning in the story to provide numerous applications and insights. Perhaps most significant is the role of the father, which helps us understand God and how He relates to us. Viewed through a paternal lens the parable illustrates the goodness of God rather than the sinfulness of the son.

Often we perceive a contrast between the nature and character of God in the Old Testament in comparison with the New Testament. In the Old Testament, God is the Creator—distant, remote, and extraordinarily strict as seen in His punishment of Moses for striking the rock, the incineration of Nadab and Abihu for their unauthorized offering, and Uzzah for touching the Ark of the Covenant. In these accounts God is seen as unapproachable, powerful, and majestic, holy and completely "other" from us. But in the New Testament, because we have seen Jesus, we tend to view God as patient, loving, forgiving, understanding and compassionate. God has been like that from the beginning and has never changed. Thanks to Jesus, hopefully we can now believe in an image of God that reflects reality.

Jesus began the parable, "There was a man who had two sons. The younger one said to his father, 'Father, give me my share of the estate.' So he divided his property between them" (Luke 15:11–12). The younger son—clearly bored with living at home and eager to go his own way—demanded his share of the inheritance. Nothing indicates that Dad tried to convince his son of the foolishness of this course of action or of the potential for ruin. Despite his worst fears and deepest reservations, the father gave away much of his personal fortune to his younger son, knowing deep in his heart that the trajectory of his son's life would lead to tragedy.

Although the father did not hesitate to give him the money, he knew that his son lacked the maturity to set good boundaries and to handle the responsibilities of adulthood. So against the father's best parental instincts, the young man got his money—and it was party time. He took his inheritance and his possessions and hit the road to high adventure, planning never to return home again.

THE WILD SIDE

Luke 15:13 says that not long after the youth received his inheritance he spent it on "wild living." We can envision that wild living meant buying rounds of drinks for his so-called friends at the local saloon. It also may have included visiting the track, betting parlors, casinos and brothels, driving the flashiest car he could find, and dating gorgeous showgirls and models.

How popular this young man from the country became, and how quickly he hit bottom when the money disappeared. Once the cash dried up all of his "friends" deserted him, not caring whether he lived or died. They had their fun and tossed him away like the paper remains of a fast food lunch. Perhaps that was the moment of truth, when he experienced the first pangs of guilt and realized he had made a serious mistake.

As if things weren't bad enough, a famine broke out in the land and inflation grew rampant. In an effort simply to survive now that he was completely broke, this good Jewish boy hired himself out to be a keeper of pigs! At least he was given room and board, which meant a corner of the pigpen and all the slop he could fight off from the pigs.

Luke succinctly says that the youth "began to be in need" (Luke 15:14). It is amazing how quickly starvation sorts out the priorities of life. His freedom suddenly mattered very little now that he faced the prospect of a slow and painful death by starvation. The gnawing in his stomach outweighed his plan to be successful, popular and carefree. He had been so certain that all would be well, but now he was sharing a pigsty with beasts banned as "unclean" under Mosaic Law.

When many of us come to Jesus, we often find ourselves deep in the mess we have made of our lives. Rebellion lies at the root of our problems; we think that we know better than God does. It is only after we realize that we are wrong and that life in the pigsty is no life at all, that we are ready to seek Jesus and His plan of redemption.

One morning the young man awoke in the midst of a dark depression. But before he decided to end his life, the Spirit urged him to seek forgiveness from his father. With no hope of being restored to family fellowship, he envisioned rebuilding his life as one of his father's servants. "How many of my father's hired men have food to spare, and here I am starving to death! I will set out and go back to my father and say to him: Father, I have sinned against heaven and against you. I am no longer worthy to be called your son; make me like one of your hired men" (15:17–19). It must have been quite a sight to see the young man, covered with mud and reeking of pig droppings, stumbling up the road toward home, while he rehearsed his speech begging for a chance at survival.

GRACE AND MERCY

The wayward son was counting on justice to work in his favor. He thought he had blown any chance for reconciliation and that it was probably impossible to resume a normal life after making such a shambles of everything. He knew his father to be tough but fair, and he was counting on that fairness to stay alive. Although he never expected his father to respond with kindness or compassion, he depended on his father's need for an able hand to work around the farm. Even a servant-master relationship was better than no relationship at all.

The prodigal son expected, or rather hoped for, justice. Instead, he received grace and mercy, which although not mutually interchangeable, are inseparable, like two sides of the same coin. Grace gives and mercy withholds. Grace is getting what we do not deserve; mercy is *not* getting what we *do* deserve.

Meanwhile, the distraught father had been searching the horizon daily, praying that the familiar figure of his son would appear on the lane that led to home. Prayer, hope and watchfulness for the safe return of his son gave the old man a reason to live.

Long before the foul smelling, raggedy scarecrow of a man reached the front gate ready to pour out his pleas for justice, his father saw him and ran to embrace his beloved son who had been returned from death to life. Scripture says that the father was "filled with compassion" (15:20).

The love of the father had always been there, but the son could not see it until mud and hunger had shattered his reckless pride and forced open his heart and mind. Even as the father poured out his love for his wayward son, the young man still could only think about justice. The son said to his dad, "Father, I have sinned against heaven and against you. I am no longer worthy to be called your son" (15:21).

WORTHY?

But who said he had to be worthy? No one asked before he was born or while he was growing up if he was worthy or wanted to be a part of the family. It is our unworthiness to receive anything good from God, not the punishment we have so splendidly earned, that makes God's grace so marvelous, for "the gift of God is eternal life through Jesus Christ our Lord" (Rom. 3:23).

The father, far from demanding restitution for squandered funds or offering a lecture on responsibility, welcomed his son home unabashedly. He instructed the servants to draw a bath, bring a fine robe to replace his rags, shoes for his bleeding, dirty feet and a signet ring with the family crest to tangibly restore the family connection. Furthermore, he ordered the best calf to be killed and a feast prepared to celebrate the return of a loved one once mourned as dead and gone. The son that was lost was found; the son that was dead was alive (15:22–25).

Then the older brother—the good, compliant, stay-at-home one— heard the sounds of laughter and music as he returned home after a hard day in the fields. Walking in on a celebration for his rotten, low-life little brother who had come back to sponge off the old man again, he grew furious and refused to join the party (15:25–28). He must have thought either that his father preferred his younger brother or that he had some serious judgment problems.

In reality the father loved the older son as much as the younger one, if perhaps in a slightly different way. And like his little brother, the older son placed a high priority on justice. He had done all the right things, never caused his father any grief, and now, he was being treated unfairly. No one had ever thrown him a party or killed a calf for him, he whined, and he had never blown a dime of his money on liquor and prostitutes. (15:29–30).

The father tried to reassure his older son. "You are always with me, and everything I have is yours, but we had to celebrate and be glad, because this brother of yours was dead and is alive again; he was lost and is found" (15:31–32). Second chances still are rare and need to be celebrated. One son expected to be treated fairly even if it was not with affection. The other son thought he had earned his father's justice through his compliance, however grudgingly given. Neither expected to receive mercy and grace. But isn't that just like God to do the unexpected?

LOVE WITHOUT LIMITS

"The Lord is compassionate and gracious, slow to anger, abounding in love. He will not always accuse, nor will He harbor his anger forever; He does not treat us as our sins deserve or repay us according to our iniquities. For as high as the heavens are above the earth, so great is His love for those who fear Him; as far as the east is from the west, so far has He removed our transgressions from us" (Ps. 103:8–12).

The love of God the Father, as shown in His Son Jesus Christ, has been here all the time for us as well. Theologians call it prevenient grace, but we just see it as love—love that draws us from the hunger, mud, shame and bitterness of sin to a glorious homecoming. The son's bad choice landed him in the pigpen; the good decision brought him home. The message of welcome and forgiveness is there for us, too— "Get out of the pigpen of sin and come home."

The Eleventh Hour
The Penitent Thief

The best decision we can ever make involves claiming the grace and forgiveness of God and establishing an intimate relationship with the Trinity. Anything else that we believe is of value will prove worthless in light of eternity. "What will it profit a man if he gain the whole world and lose his own soul?" (Matt. 16:26).

During Jesus' brief ministry spent teaching and preaching on the Kingdom of God, He stayed open and accessible to people from all walks of life. Unlike the other religious leaders of His day, Jesus taught that salvation is not about following the law but about making our best effort, through grace, to live the life that He would live in our place. Over time this kind of intentional discipleship slowly leads to a changed heart, which ultimately enables us to routinely carry out the most important commandment in the law, "Love the Lord your God and your neighbor as yourself." Salvation, or eternal living, is about working jointly with God—individually and as a community—to undercut evil with good in the kingdom of God. In the book of Acts the early Apostles focus not on the cross but on the resurrection and the eternal spiritual life, or "Zoe," in Greek, that is available through Jesus Christ. Christ offers us the gift of Zoe right here and now; we do not have to wait until we die and go to heaven to make Jesus' divine love and power a part of us.

RIGHTEOUSNESS

While delivering His longest uninterrupted discourse in what has come to be called, "The Sermon on the Mount," Jesus pointed to the Pharisees and told the assembled throng, "For I tell you that unless your righteousness surpasses that of the Pharisees and teachers of the law, you will certainly not enter the kingdom of heaven" (Matt. 5:21).

How could anyone's righteousness possibly ever exceed that of the Pharisees? They were the all time award winners of righteousness by good works who slavishly adhered to a set of minute rules. If we pastors and laypeople have to do better than the Pharisees, what chance do any of us have to enter the kingdom of God? If salvation is based on our good works and adherence to rules, we have no chance.

It is impossible to be good enough to enter the kingdom because sin makes us "bad to the bone." Paul says the same thing in Ephesians 2:8–9: "For it is by grace you have been saved, through faith—and this not from yourselves, it is the gift of God—not by works, so that no one can boast." We can't ever be good enough to earn forgiveness, heaven and eternal life. The only thing we are worthy of is the judgment of God. But grace is the free, unmerited, favor of God that can never be earned or repaid.

Jesus was put to death on a cross between two criminals (Luke 23:32). It appears that these two criminals were being executed for their crime—robbery, murder, insurrection, or arson. So, if these two men were thieves, why not cut off a hand to teach them a lesson? At worst, they were strong enough and expendable enough to be chained to an oar on a galley or condemned to a life of hard labor. Slaves were valuable. The Romans did not waste cheap, disposable manpower by putting people to death. They would no more waste a good slave than we would enter a Rolls Royce in a demolition derby today.

These two felons must have been so wicked that the Romans concluded they were beyond rehabilitation. They were so evil and posed such a threat to life and property that they could not even live in a slave society.

One of the criminals next to Jesus shouted over the din, "Aren't you the Christ? Save yourself and us." The other replied with uncharacteristic penitence given his fate and arrest history. "Don't you fear God, since you are under the same sentence? We are punished justly, for what our deeds deserve. But this man has done nothing wrong."

"REMEMBER ME"

"Jesus," he continued, "remember me when you come into your kingdom."

Jesus replied through His own pain and anguish, "I tell you the truth, today you will be with me in paradise" (Luke 23:32–43).

This brief exchange helps us understand the context and application of grace and the significance of choosing life in Christ. The penitent thief did not have to know about redemption and salvation theology before accepting Christ and His grace. He did not need to be bombarded with more than 2,000 years of church history and doctrine any more than he needed to know the subtle differences between denominations. He did not even need to know the as-yet unwritten Scripture that says, "God demonstrates His own love for us in this: While we were still sinners, Christ died for us" (Rom. 5:8). He just knew, deep in his heart, after all the excuses and rationalizations were swept away and he faced imminent death and eternal judgment, that Jesus was true. He was to be trusted and His message of grace was real.

The dying thief got it right on the first try, for he claimed no record of church attendance, history of good works, or responsible behavior. If anything his life had been misspent and squandered in crime. He had absolutely nothing to bargain with, yet he went home with the pearl of great price. In those long hours of agony, perhaps he recalled the words that Jesus spoke one afternoon on a hillside, "Seek first the kingdom of God and His righteousness, and all these things will be given to you as well" (Matt. 6:33). Those added things were forgiveness and heaven. Nothing in the thief's request or Jesus' reply mentioned Holy Communion or baptism—both rituals of debate and dispute that have been extraordinarily divisive over the centuries. By asking for forgiveness and trusting Jesus to do as He promised, the thief received everything he needed.

As the lyrics to a song by the Rolling Stones tell us about making decisions,

"You can't always get what you want,
You can't always get what you want,
But if you try sometimes,
You just might find
You get what you need."

And what you and I need is GRACE. What an excellent choice—none better. What choice will you make?

CREST 🛡 BOOKS

Salvation Army National Publications

Crest Books, a division of The Salvation Army's National Publications department, was established in 1997 so contemporary Salvationist voices could be captured and bound in enduring form for future generations, to serve as witnesses to the continuing force and mission of the Army.

Shaw Clifton, *Never the Same Again: Encouragement for new and not-so-new Christians*, 1997

Christmas Through the Years: A War Cry Treasury (Compilation), 1997

William Francis, *Celebrate the Feasts of the Lord: The Christian Heritage of the Sacred Jewish Festivals*, 1998

Marlene Chase, *Pictures from the Word*, 1998

Joe Noland, *A Little Greatness*, 1998

Lyell M. Rader, *Romance & Dynamite: Essays on Science and the Nature of Faith*, 1998

Shaw Clifton, *Who Are These Salvationists?: An Analysis for the 21st Century*, 1999

Easter Through the Years: A War Cry Treasury, (Compilation), 1999

Terry Camsey, *Slightly Off Center! Growth Principles to Thaw Frozen Paradigms*, 2000

Philip Needham, *He Who Laughed First: Delighting in a Holy God*, (in collaboration with Beacon Hill Press, Kansas City), 2000

Henry Gariepy (ed.), *A Salvationist Treasury: 365 Devotional Meditations from the Classics to the Contemporary*, 2000

Marlene Chase, *Our God Comes: And Will Not Be Silent*, 2001

A. Kenneth Wilson, *Fractured Parables: And Other Tales to Lighten the Heart and Quicken the Spirit*, 2001

Carroll Ferguson Hunt, *If Two Shall Agree* (in collaboration with Beacon Hill Press, Kansas City), 2001

John C. Izzard, *Pen of Flame: The Life and Poetry of Catherine Baird*, 2002

Henry Gariepy, *Andy Miller: A Legend and a Legacy*, 2002

A Word in Season: A Collection of Short Stories, (Compilation), 2002

R. David Rightmire, *Sanctified Sanity: The Life and Teaching of Samuel Logan Brengle*, 2003

Chick Yuill, *Leadership on the Axis of Change*, 2003

Living Portraits Speaking Still: A Collection of Bible Studies (Compilation), 2004

A. Kenneth Wilson, *The First Dysfunctional Family: A Modern Guide to the Book of Genesis*, 2004

Allen Satterlee, *Turning Points: How The Salvation Army Found a Different Path*, 2004

David Laeger, *Shadow and Substance: The Tabernacle of the Human Heart*, 2005

Check Yee, *Good Morning China*, 2005

Marlene Chase, *Beside Still Waters: Great Prayers of the Bible for Today*, 2005

Roger J. Green, *The Life & Ministry of William Booth* (in collaboration with Abingdon Press, Nashville), 2006

Norman H. Murdoch, *Soldiers of the Cross: Susie Swift and David Lamb,* 2006

Henry Gariepy, *Israel L. Gaither: Man with a Mission*, 2006

R.G. Moyles, ed., *I Knew William Booth*, 2007

John Larsson, *Saying Yes to Life*, 2007

Frank Duracher, *Smoky Mountain High*, 2007

R.G. Moyles, *Come Join Our Army*, 2008

Ken Elliott, *The Girl Who Invaded America: The Odyssey Of Eliza Shirley*, 2008

Ed Forster, *101 Everyday Sayings From the Bible*, 2008

Harry Williams, *An Army Needs An Ambulance Corps: A History of The Salvation Army's Medical Services,* 2009

Judith L. Brown and Christine Poff, eds., *No Longer Missing: Compelling True Stories from The Salvation Army's Missing Persons Ministry*, 2009

Quotes of the Past & Present (Compilation from the War Cry), 2009

Henry Gariepy and Stephen Court, *Hallmarks of The Salvation Army,* 2010

John Cheydleur and Ed Forster, eds., *Every Sober Day Is a Miracle*, 2010

R.G. Moyles, *William Booth in America: Six Visits 1886 - 1907*, 2010

Shaw Clifton, *Selected Writings, Vol. 1: 1974-1999 and Vol. 2: 2000-2010,* 2010

How I Met The Salvation Army, (Compilation from the War Cry), 2011